Selected Stories

Selected STORIES

CHARLES MANGEL

SELECTED STORIES

iUniverse books may be ordered through booksellers or by contacting:

iUniverse
1663 Liberty Drive
Bloomington, IN 47403
www.iuniverse.com
1-800-Authors (1-800-288-4677)

Because of the dynamic nature of the Internet, any web addresses or links contained in this book may have changed since publication and may no longer be valid. The views expressed in this work are solely those of the author and do not necessarily reflect the views of the publisher, and the publisher hereby disclaims any responsibility for them.

Any people depicted in stock imagery provided by Thinkstock are models, and such images are being used for illustrative purposes only. Certain stock imagery © Thinkstock.

ISBN: 978-1-4917-4416-1 (sc)
ISBN: 978-1-4917-4424-6 (hc)
ISBN: 978-1-4917-4417-8 (e)

Library of Congress Control Number: 2014914770

Printed in the United States of America.

iUniverse rev. date: 11/24/2014

For Bob Meskill and Marty Gansberg,
teachers and friends

and for....

June, Howard, Cindy, Debbie, Arne, Beth, Matt, Allen, Felicia, Nicole, Jason, Kirsten

and

Rob, Kaitlyn, Jonathan, Alyssa, Daniel, Jesse, Rebecca, Emma, Joshua, Hayley Rose

CONTENTS

HOW TO MAKE A CRIMINAL OUT OF A CHILD

BY CHARLES MANGEL
LOOK SENIOR EDITOR

"I can't send him back to his whore of a mother. His school has thrown him out. He has done nothing more than try to run away from his miserable home. All I can offer this child is a jail."

—*Magistrate David S. Schaffer,*
Chicago Juvenile Court

As I write this, some 100,000 children are sitting in jails and jail-like institutions throughout the country. They are as young as six. Most, perhaps 60 percent, are not delinquents. They have committed *no criminal acts.*

They are in trouble with their schools or victims of bad homes or no homes or runaways or emotionally disturbed or mentally retarded or neurologically impaired.

But they are in jails (thousands of them illegally, without benefit of court hearings or attorneys or specific release dates) because there is no place else for them to be. These jails, which have many different names—detention center, training school, even hospital—have guards and locks and, for the most part, bars and high walls.

They put Bernie in one of these jails at age six. Because that's when, as far as officials were concerned, he began to mess up.

Poster-attractive except for a pair of the most badly crossed eyes I have ever seen, Bernie was picked up by a Chicago cop one cool fall midnight wandering barefoot around a subway station.

He was already a veteran runaway and a panhandler. Lost among nine—soon to be ten—kids, a semiliterate, rarely working father, a childlike mother, he took to the streets at four. He was hit by cars twice that first year, suffering a fractured skull both times.

The policeman took Bernie to the Audy Home that night, shortly after his sixth birthday. (The Audy Home is a jail for children.) He was sent home the next day, turned over to his parents and ordered to report to school. Kindergarten.

He refused to attend. Disheveled, dirty, butt of jokes for his crossed eyes, which were never treated, he skipped 31 of his first 40 days. That set the pattern for the next four years. Bernie was to spend almost two of those years in Audy on five different stays.

Continuing to run and to get picked up, he shuttled between his home, a urine-reeking, rag-strewn three rooms, five sets of foster parents and, inevitably, when things fell apart, Audy. After years of being responsible to no one, he was hard to control; each foster home quickly threw him back.

Because he was so handsome—ash-brown hair, blue eyes, a quiet smile—he became a favorite among the staff at Audy. Everyone felt badly that he was disintegrating.

Like all cities in this country, Chicago offers little treatment for children who need help—but lots of testing. During his repeated confinements at Audy, Bernie was frequently evaluated. Tested there for the first time at age six, he was found to be of normal intelligence.

By age eight, the examining psychologist could report: "His contact with his environment has decreased." By nine: "Bernie is getting depressed. [He is] beginning to withdraw severely." The next year: "It is quite possible he is deteriorating due to lack of special academic compensation [and] experiencing extreme emotional regression."

Several doctors recommended a boarding home and school where Bernie could get the attention and firm guidance he desperately needed. "Unfortunately," noted one laconic report in Bernie's ninth year, "such an environment was not obtainable for him." Illinois, like most states, pays $3,000 to $8,000 per year for each troubled child it is able to place in private residential schools. But these schools reserve the right to turn down anyone they believe would not fit into their program. Illinois has no say. Eight schools refused Bernie. Public residential schools for long-term stays do not exist.

The rejection from the foster homes "rendered Bernie ... chaotic," reported one psychologist. Back home, Bernie's parents often locked him in a closet to keep him from running, and moved frequently to evade juvenile authorities.

At ten, Bernie became, in the eyes of the law, a delinquent.

He wanted a bike. So he took one, menacing a boy with a small penknife. He was returned to Audy. He was now functioning at the level of a retarded child. His IQ had plummeted 30 points. He had spent three weeks of the prior 52 in his neighborhood school. He could not read, write, tell time. He was drifting away from the world.

The inevitable test: He was now retarded, it said. The court promptly and officially labeled him that, even though a physician two years earlier had said emphatically: "He is not retarded." (If Bernie was in fact retarded at that point, he had joined a large group. The President's Committee on Mental Retardation estimates that three out of four of the six million retarded in this country *were born with healthy minds.* Their retardation, like Bernie's, was caused by the failure of our society to provide what a child needs to survive.) Bernie—age ten—was ordered to a state institution for the retarded. Commented a probation officer, "He will never come out."

Bernie's parents, meanwhile, had had enough of Chicago. They wanted to move to a relative's farm in rural Florida. Almost as an afterthought, the day before they were to leave, they asked if Bernie could come with them. He was released. The only thing Chicago and Illinois could figure out for Bernie was to let him go. Saved from a cage for the retarded, he is now back where the problem began.

Bernie spent almost half of four crucial years in a city detention center. Harry is farther along. Harry was 14, looked 12 and, when I first saw him, he was in solitary confinement in Illinois' maximum-security prison for juveniles--a penitentiary for children.

His major crime: an inability to control himself.

Slight, blond hair hanging over his forehead in bangs, he could be heard shrieking through the prison building when we entered. "Damned food; damned slop they give us…. Hey, who's out there … ?" As photographer Charles Harbutt and I approached and began to talk with him, he quieted down. He wanted attention.

Harry had been a problem "since he was nine months old," his mother later told me. He destroyed "every toy he owned" in fits of temper. Extremely bright, he had a low frustration level and would explode "without warning" when he didn't succeed immediately at anything he wanted to do. Even before he started to talk, he would grab a household "weapon"—a vase, a broom—when provoked by one of his brothers or sisters.

Harry's mother, a good-hearted divorcee concerned about her seven children, married an older man who wanted to take care of his new family, but who quickly admitted defeat with Harry. Although obviously bright, Harry could not be controlled at home or in school. He tore apart his classes and virtually destroyed his family.

He walked into a liquor store at age 11 and stole several cartons of cigarettes. He didn't smoke and didn't try to sell them. He apparently just wanted to boast. That same day, as a friend was set upon by two boys, Harry waded in and got so angry that he pulled out a pocketknife and stabbed one of the boys in the shoulder. (When I asked him why, he replied: "I just got mad.")

For the last two incidents, the court ordered him to a training school. Paroled 15 months later, he was wilder than ever. He lasted three months at home.

His parole was revoked. He went back to the training school, was so incorrigible that he was transferred to the maximum-security school in the Illinois system. (In any state in this nation, a child who is, for example, a runaway, can, by just running repeatedly, promote himself into a maximum-security cell. He is, thus, controlled.) Unable to stop lashing out at virtually everyone around him, Harry spent most of his time in solitary confinement, a five-by-ten-foot cell. Of the three months following my visit, he spent 71 days locked up alone. When he was particularly troublesome, the "cage men" (or "control men") injected him, forcibly if necessary, with Thorazine. Thorazine is a powerful tranquilizer. It is commonly used in the treatment of psychotics. No physician termed Harry psychotic. The cage men used the drug to keep him groggy. A prescription—a technical requirement—was routinely provided. "One injection," the then superintendent told me, "often kept him out six hours."

Harry was examined by a psychiatrist who reported: "This is a ... helpless little boy confused and overwhelmed by his impulses and environment. The next few years could be crucial as to whether he goes into irreversible personal disorder." The psychiatrist asked that Harry be given a medical evaluation and then treatment based on those findings. Four months later, the medical evaluations had not been scheduled. The same psychiatrist saw Harry again, and again recommended the examination. He noted: "His behavior has deteriorated. His prognosis is poorer."

I took my notebooks to a pediatrician who specializes in learning and behavior problems in children. He suspected, based on what I could tell him, that Harry has suffered since birth from a combination of primarily physical—*not emotional*—problems. They made it impossible for him to control himself without the right medical help, which no one had given him.

What happens to a boy who grows into manhood in a jail?

Chuck Paulson is 35. He has spent 26 years in some kind of institution. He has been a burglar, an armed robber and, almost, a murderer. When I interviewed him, he had just been released from a penitentiary in an Eastern state. He had been out ten months, the longest period of time he had been free *since he was seven years old*.

"My mother put me in an orphanage when I was seven," he recalled. Why? "I don't know. My parents were both working. I was an only child. I don't think they wanted me around. They were both pretty young."

Chuck kept runningg away, trying to go home to his parents. After three years, the orphanage gave up and sent him back. But he didn't want to go to school. While truant one day, he wandered into a variety store, picked up a hard-boiled Easter egg from a display and ate it. A neighbor told his mother.

The next day, Chuck's mother petitioned the court to have him committed as an uncontrollable child. (In many states, "incorrigible" children, solely on petition of a parent, school or police official, can be held until age 21. New Jersey last year imprisoned a boy until newspaper publicity forced his release. He was five.) Chuck, 12, was sent to a reformatory. He was to stay there for most of the next four years. He had done nothing more serious than eat the egg and play hooky.

"When you go into reform school at 12 or so," he told me, "and you see a guy maybe a year or two older in there for robbing, he's a big man. You look up to him. You listen to him. I listened to stories about jobs. I just took it all in my head."

"What did you learn?"

"I learned the best time to break into a market, how to get into a closed gas station, how to empty a jewelry-store window, how to find out if a house is empty and get in quietly, how to sell the junk you steal." (Eight out of ten kids—*including those who enter these institutions for non-delinquent behavior*—commit crimes after they leave. Three out of four are back in jail within five years.)

After a year at the reformatory, Chuck got a two-week home leave. He could barely wait to test his new knowledge. "I hitchhiked across the state line the first night out—they told me not to mess with your hometown—and crashed into two closed gas stations. I went into the cash registers and the vending machines. I still remember, I got $50 in one and $20 in the second. That was big money for me. I was 13 and a half. I hit two more when that money ran out. Now *I* had some stories to tell when my leave was up."

Chuck learned "how to stick a knife in a guy, shoot a gun. They taught me to fight; they made me want to do it, to get revenge. The kids said if you've got the guts to stick it into a guy, then you're OK. Otherwise, you're a punk. This went on, day after day. All we did was talk. They had pictures of guns and showed us how to load them, use them. Over and over. When I got out and got a gun, I felt at home with it."

Chuck saw his first gang rape in the reformatory. "A thin, blond kid hung with me, and I watched out for him. One day, 16 bigger guys caught him alone and raped him in a classroom, beat him silly. I saw 12- and 13-year-old kids rape eight-year-olds. I saw a gym master rape a kid in an empty swimming pool.

"Everybody does it. Anyone who's in prison for any time and says he doesn't do it—by consent or force—is a liar."

("Almost every slightly built young man is sexually approached within hours after his admission…," one investigator told a Senate subcommittee. "Many are … repeatedly raped by gangs of aggressors. Can anyone of us understand what degradation and hatred a young man must feel when he is released into the community after being homosexually raped?")

Discharged at 14, Chuck formed a three-boy gang and started breaking into houses. "We would do 12 to 15 houses in an afternoon when people were out."

His career had begun. It was to take him into four different reformatories, federal and state prisons, through five knifings of other inmates—he tried to kill each, but failed—through episodes with drugs. When discharged the last time, he had been out of confinement a total of 13 days in 13 and a half years. Now he sat with me, worrying about his future.

He had lost five jobs because his employers learned he is an ex-convict; another because of his temper. Although he is trying to stay clean, he had broken into two houses the week before we talked. He is trying to stay off pills and liquor but may be losing. He is continually looking over his shoulder, afraid he'll be caught for those entries, dodging friends he made in prison who are looking for him so they can get back to the only real work any of them knows. "I get two or three offers a week."

Chuck doesn't know what he will do. He has the defenses of a child. "He is terror-stricken," a new friend of his told me. "He carries a knife because he's afraid someone will stab him in the back. He doesn't know how to trust. He doesn't believe anyone could love him. He tried to con me until he realized I wasn't out to hurt him, that I wanted to help. He doesn't know what it is to be happy."

The only thing Chuck is sure about is "that it started in reform school. That's trade school, that's where I learned it all." He pleads: "Stop reform schools. Eight out of ten guys I saw in prison were in reform school with me."

Bernie, Harry and Chuck Paulson are not isolated examples. They represent dozens of boys and girls I met across the country, non-delinquent or borderline delinquent children who are committed to institutions for indeterminate stays under the guise of treatment. But only five out of 100 get it.

Instead, they find themselves in a world governed by brutality (one survey reported major physical punishment in two out of three institutions) and a different code of conduct. "Imagine," said one researcher, "what can happen to a ten-year-old boy, whose only offense is having been deserted by his parents, when he is assigned a bed between a burglar and a homicide suspect." Inevitably, they learn a new set of rules.

No one, anywhere, demands an accounting of what happens to these children. Nobody touches their lives. Except on a hit-or-miss basis, no hand exists to support a stumbling child, no hand exists to help good families that find survival impossible without assistance. I interviewed poor parents of disturbed or brain-injured kids who committed their children in desperation because they could find no other promise of treatment. Each "incorrigible" child went to jail. None got the promised treatment. Schools simply eject kids who do not learn—90,000 under 16 walk the streets all day in New York City, 60,000 in Philadelphia, 36,000 in Detroit, 53,000 in Los Angeles.

The glut of public and private social-service agencies allows children and their families to fall between them because no one agency, anywhere, is responsible for anyone. *Six* different Chicago agencies had a shot at Bernie during his four years; his probation-department social worker and his school social worker had never contacted each other to discuss his problems. I asked his probation-department social worker what she did for him. "I visited him and I brought him apples," she said. "He loved apples."

Most judges refuse to visit institutions they sentence kids to. Three out of four juvenile courts have neither diagnostic services to seek out reasons for a child's behavior nor treatment services to help a child *before* committing him to an institution.

Logic plays little part in our treatment of children in trouble. We imprison a child of seven and tell ourselves *he* is the failure. We maintain we will treat him, but only one of 20 institution employees is assigned to rehabilitation. We worry about the rising rate of crime and acknowledge that serious juvenile crime is up 78 percent (half of all major crimes are committed by juveniles), yet our federal government spends $480 million for an omnibus crime act, and only $14.7 million for delinquency prevention—versus $4.4 billion for highway construction. We complain endlessly about money, yet we will spend as high as $12,000 to keep one child in a jail cell for one year when most could be helped in small group homes for a third of that sum. "Secure institutions are necessary for only some ten percent who are dangerous," says Milton Rector of the National Council on Crime and Delinquency.

We know our juvenile prisons are failures, yet we plan to increase their capacities by almost 50 percent. We deplore the need to put non-delinquents with hardcore child criminals—and some 10,000 in with *adult* prisoners—yet unblushingly continue to do it. In 1961, New York state passed a law forbidding non-delinquents to be placed in facilities housing delinquents. The jails started to empty. Suddenly there was no need for all those guards. Forty percent were let go. They protested. The legislators repealed the law and returned to the old system.

As a national community, we know how to identify many kids who are likely to get into trouble by the time they reach the third grade. We are beginning to understand that many children who misbehave flagrantly—perhaps as many as half of them—have basic medical problems that if treated would allow them to control weird impulses that lead to assaults, even murder. We have watched experiments in rehabilitation (Illinois among the outstanding ones) that indicate promising ways to reduce repeater rates—and costs—dramatically.

Yet we pass all this by as if it does not exist. "Why are we so willing to give up on the child in trouble?" asks Lois Forer in *No One Will Lissen*. "There are two possible reasons. The first is that we don't want to help; the second, that we don't believe we *can* help. We know that the children who suffer from lack of facilities are primarily poor children—black, Puerto Rican, Indian, deprived—in short, *not our children*."

Few people feel any sense of outrage. I met in Chicago with a group of lawyers, judges and social workers who spend their days working with children in court. They impressed me as decent men and women. They uttered all the right words. But they spoke with a curious hollowness of feeling. As the evening wore on, I found myself being grateful that the future of my children did not depend on their concern.

"The way things are now, it is probably better for all concerned if young delinquents were not detected," says Milton Luger, former director of the New York State Division for Youth. "Too many of them get worse in our care." Not one state in this country, adds the National Council, is doing a proper job of rehabilitating kids in trouble.

We are a slipshod people. We tend to do nothing unless a crisis is at hand, and then we seek simplistic, temporary measures. We wrap ourselves in our comforts, tend to think the universe is where we are and blink at those who are cold, hungry, sick, in trouble. It appears the time of slippage may be ending. The time may be beginning when, compassion and purity of purpose aside, *we* are going to be hurt significantly if we don't reach out to those aliens who dare not to be self-sufficient. "If you are among brigands and you are silent, you are a brigand yourself," a folk saying goes. Civilization is not a matter of museums and global communications. It derives from a quality of mind and of concern. And by that definition, we, of course, are not a civilized nation at all, rather a self-centered, stupid one. And the soothing words of all our politicians, all our churchmen, all our "important" people matter not. We are incompetent.

About a month before I reached Los Angeles during the research for this story, a nine-year-old named Teddy had run from his mother there. An alcoholic, she used to leave him alone for days at a time. He was a chronic truant and had begun to mug smaller kids. A policeman showed me his farewell note: "Mom, I am sorry but you do not care about me so I have to leave you. I don't care no more. I had to go begging for food. I cannot go begging no more. Love, Teddy." The boy added an afterthought: "How am I going to live? Can you tell me that?"

END

PINOCCHIO LIVES!

BY CHARLES MANGEL
LOOK SENIOR EDITOR

HE STANDS THERE for a flash, his face framed by the flapping blue curtain. Then he rushes onto the floor, waddling, feet jabbing in different directions, the celebrated nose leading the boiled-shirt front, tiny eyes peeking from layers of folded skin, mouth puckered like a goldfish, face quivering.

"Ya gotta start off each day wid a song." The number lasts 15 minutes, lyrics interspersed with cracks as the music dips and swells to surround the one-liners ("Da music covers da bombs"). He is never still, and the audience has little chance to be quiet. He fires out something for all of them, and the bombs *are* covered, not just by musical fortissimos but by a wink, a shrug, a despairing sigh as this little man considers the gall of intruders trying, ever trying, to get into his act.

Durante is old now. His face is permanently subdivided by ravines that seem to radiate from the well-publicized extension in its center. But the skills that first drew people to him in a Coney Island saloon in 1910 still work. Durante continues to play Durante, a warm, good, oppressed, not fully lettered man in whom everyone can see a bit of himself. He is a throwback. In a day when entertainment is a prefabricated commodity and we are told performers are stars before we even know their skills, Durante raucously reminds us of a time when entertainers were fun, genuine, alive. More than Durante's nose relates him to the storied wooden boy, Pinocchio. They share the same impish, wondering quality.

The show is over. Durante, 76 this month, has been racing across the floor for most of an hour. He closes to a standing ovation. Behind him, over-dressed matrons, bare-kneed teens howl for more. Backstage, he slumps for a moment, growls at a busboy: "I seen ya lookin' at dose girls while Durante was workin'," and leaves as the youngster dissolves into giggles.

In his suite upstairs at Washington's Shoreham Hotel, he moves quickly from damp tuxedo to a disreputable blue terrycloth robe he refuses to abandon. Ron Serafino, his batman, begins his ministrations. First, cornflakes (Durante ate them long before he began to sell the product on TV) then some toast (*lightly* browned). It's early into the next day. Durante will prowl restlessly until 4 or 5 a.m., when he finally will drop off. Jack Roth, his drummer since 1920, sits by his side reading a newspaper until he sleeps. Then Roth goes quietly to his own room.

Little has changed in the man who refused for the first 13 years of his career, to talk to the audience from his piano stool for fear "dey would laugh at me." Now, they do indeed laugh, but it's not the kind of amusement Durante had feared. I saw this the first time I visited him in Del Mar, Calif., where he spends every summer with his wife Marge and their seven-year-old adopted daughter Cecilia ("Call her CeCe or ya'll answer to Durante"). He asked me to drive him to the supermarket. Dressed rather routinely between the fedora and an old pair of brown oxfords unencumbered by laces, he padded the aisles looking for items on the list supplied by his wife. Worrying that I might feel left out, Durante provided accompaniment: "Ya gotta watch da values. Dese napkins are three cents off. That's how ya shop. Another place offers four cents off, dat's where I go. Where's da bread? Where do dey hide da bread?" As his arms filled up, "Where's da wheelbarrow [cart]?" He consulted with the butcher about two spring chickens: "Turn dem over. Let me see da bottoms." Mission accomplished, Durante advanced to the checkout counter, paid, signed four autographs (there seemed to be no shortage of assistants at that one counter), headed the "wheelbarrow" out to the car, then slapped his forehead. He dashed back to the counter: "I'll get killed by Marge! Where's da stamps?"

He pushed the wagon through the lot, inadvertently forcing a beer truck to stop. The driver grumped, then recognized: "Hiya, Jimmy." He hopped out: "Need a hand?" Durante waved at me: "Naw, thanks, brought m' secretary." The driver scowled at me, told Jimmy his wife had asked to be remembered to him and bounded back into the cab. Jimmy was accosted four more times in a 30-yard walk to the car. Each person talked to him as a friend and departed grinning.

Durante understands pain. Knowing it, he is patient with people, even the pushers and shovers who believe that an entertainer is permanently on display. He was a small ugly kid on New York's jumbled Lower East Side, and things didn't always break right for him. He once told a writer he was "a shrinkin' violence.... Those pimples ... those little eyes. Every time I went down the street I'd hear, 'Lookit, the big-nose kid!' And when anybody'd stare, I'd just sneak off. Even if they said nothin', ... I'd shrivel up and think they was sayin', 'What a ugly kid! What a monster!' ... Even when I am makin' a fortune on account of the big beak, and while I am out there on the stage laughin' and kiddin' about the nose, at no time was I ever happy about it." The fear of ridicule that kept Durante tongue-tied lasted into the days of Clayton, Jackson and Durante in the twenties. Lou Clayton, a tough ex-vaudeville dancer who fiercely loved Durante, made him get on the floor and clown. Years later, when asked why he never poked fun at people in his routines, Durante replied, "Make fun? Wid dis schnozz of mine? Everyone's got a schnozz somewhere, so who can make fun of dem?"

Durante's unfailing good nature ("You can warm your hands on this man," Clayton once said) and simplicity draw people to him. Traveling with him is paradise. Everyone smiles. Several hundred visitors touring Washington's Capitol deserted their guides one morning when they saw Durante quietly walking through the Rotunda. They locked him in their center. Few asked for autographs. Most just wanted to greet him. An elderly grandfather in a California restaurant one evening had a waiter ask Durante if he would accept a drink, later thanked Jimmy "for entertaining us for so many years." At meal's end, the owner of the restaurant laughed when Durante asked for the check: "Anyone who charges Jimmy Durante for a meal should be put in jail."

Many entertainers fall when new generations grow into strength. Durante gathers newcomers to him. At a recent college benefit, bead-wearing students deserted a performing rock 'n' roll group when they heard Durante was there. Some days later, as Durante was experimenting with a song in his living room—*"Sometimes the cold gets in my bones; sometimes the night comes down on me"*—a lovely young visitor, perhaps 18, whispered: "He's beautiful."

Durante remembers the bleakness of inactivity (during the final illness of his first wife—the Mrs. Calabash of TV farewells—he worked little for four years). So he will not retire: "It almost killed Jolson before that movie brought him back. I'd die if that phone stopped ringing. I don't need da money, but I do need da work." The phone doesn't stop ringing. His nightclub dates, the bulk of his schedule, keep him traveling about 20 weeks each year. Durante turns down more work than he accepts. There could be enough to keep him traveling 52 weeks a year, including a weekly TV series next season.

I asked him if he were content, if there was anything more he wanted. Yes: "I hope I live till CeCe marries. I don't want anything else. I've got my family, my health. I thank God every morning for both. I like to make people laugh. Dey like me. What could I want? I don't want all da money in da world."

Durante's act is humor and clowning, bits with pretty young ladies in abbreviated costumes, mock arguments with talented Sonny King, his singing partner and foil, duets with Eddie Jackson, his friend since 1916. But the high point for each audience inevitably comes when the clowning stops and Durante sits at a piano and the lights go down and the small man with the nose and the hat and the cigar sings a ballad. Usually, it's *Young at Heart*. Sometimes, it's *September Song*. And sometimes, in slow tempo, it's another, a trademark:

"Who will be with you when I'm far away
When I'm far, far away from you?"

END

THE DISAPPEARING WORLD
OF A NEW YORK JEW

BY CHARLES MANGEL
LOOK SENIOR EDITOR

DEATH IS A SLOW INTRUDER. *Even to the man who falls dead in midstride, it began—when? When an artery wall began to thicken? When a virus became implanted? On the day he left his mother's body? Death, to a synagogue, comes slowly too. And who knows its start? A man dies. A family moves. A son forgets. Suddenly, the seats, once filled twice daily, grow thick with dust. And only the old people are left. A neighborhood has changed.*

The decay of New York's tenemented South Bronx laps at the Intervale Jewish Center: dog droppings on the front steps, a chalked "Jews next" on the sidewalk, the vacant stares of neighbors as they walk by. A small group of the Jewish elderly—their number swelling briefly as survivors straggle in from deserted synagogues nearby, diminishing as others move—holds out against the tide.

The South Bronx, like Harlem and Brownsville, is the newly abandoned intersection that paths which began in Europe touched briefly before radiating toward Westchester, Long Island, Connecticut. After a quarter-century in the Bronx, Harry Kirschner, 86, falteringly old, ill, introduced to flight as a police-beaten boy of 14 in Russia, refuses to move again.

The first time I saw him, he was wheeling a once-elegant high-bodied pram—the kind associated with the east side of Central Park and snobbish governesses—through the garbage-thick streets, a slight, bent, Orthodox Jew looking for the minutiae of junk that provided his living.

15

Alone and uncomprehending in a community that had passed him, he clung desperately to what he knew, still working and still praying to the one God he was introduced to 80 winters before in a small, bare iceberg of a Hebrew school.

His dreams have altered many times since then, but his God remains constant, the only constant he has ever known. Encroaching blindness and the pleas of his wife have since forced him to stop maneuvering his pram through the vicious traffic of city streets. His synagogue is his last stronghold.

So he sits, alone on a synagogue bench built for seven, and he waits, hopefully, for nine more men to come so Sabbath prayers can begin.

The battle for survival that Jews have fought so many times is now being lost in the South Bronx. Of 24 Orthodox synagogues in the immediate area, only Intervale, one of the plainest, is still open. The closest active one is about a mile away, a long walk for an aging Orthodox Jew who will not ride on the Sabbath or major holy days.

The change has been swift. The Bronx, once a kind of material new Jerusalem for Jews, is a haven no longer.

"When we moved here in 1940," Harry Kirschner remembers, "we couldn't find two empty seats for Yom Kippur. There were *schuls* [synagogues] everywhere we looked."

A meeting called recently of those who pray at Intervale drew five people, three of them women, and the youngest of them all 69. Dues are no longer collected for fear they will drive away poor worshipers; charity has to pay the bills. There is no president, for there is no willing man young enough to take the job. A determined woman, widow of the last president, handles what affairs there are.

"On Simchas Torah," Harry Kirschner says, "you had to get in line to dance with the Torah." (The holiday, "the Rejoicing of the Torah," is the happiest in the Hebrew calendar; it marks the completion of the yearlong reading of the Torah, the five books of Moses, core of Jewish scripture, and the start again at Genesis.) "Officers wore tuxedoes to services on the important holidays. We had weddings and bar mitzvahs. Herman Wouk was bar mitzvah'd here. We even danced in the street."

Stripped cars have claimed the streets around the basement

synagogue. Inside, the old flooring is warped and crudely patched in places, prayer shawls are frayed, and the mismatched *siddurim* (prayer books) tell silently of their earlier service in other places, now abandoned. An old, valuable brass "curtain," which divided the men's and women's sections (the sexes pray separately in an Orthodox synagogue) was stolen several years ago; a cheap white-cotton drape makes do.

"Plenty of men and boys came for morning and evening prayers. Who ever thought of hoodlums here?" Harry Kirschner asks quietly.

Only two police precincts of New York's 77 exceed Intervale's for crime. Vandals invaded the synagogue three times the week before the High Holidays in the fall of 1967. Torah scrolls were broken, stripped of their thin silver ornaments and cloth coverings and thrown onto the floor; prayer books and drapes were ripped; and paint was splashed around. Police caught two of the vandals on their way out; one was 13 years old.

Faced by increasing pressures from the neighborhood, a strong group within the synagogue tried five years ago to close the building. Harry Kirschner and others asked a simple question: "What will happen to the Jews who still want to pray?" They won their point.

No community of religious Jews can exist without a synagogue. School and house of worship both (it was born as a school before it made room for the worshipers), the *schul* allows the devout to function. It must be open every day to enable those who can, after morning worship, to pore over the law. It allows the pious, given a *minyan*, the quorum of ten needed for formal prayer, to read the Torah and say the memorial *kaddish* for those close kin who have died.

The children's school at Intervale went first. By 1964, the congregation could no longer afford a full-time rabbi, and decided to hire one just for the holidays. By last year, that job was turned over to an itinerant cantor. Morning and evening services faded away as elderly men found it difficult to face both the night and the worry of the streets. A membership list, mainstay of any organization, no longer exists. Any Jew who comes to Intervale to pray is a member for as long as he wishes to be one.

Harry Kirschner, perhaps alone, somehow hopes for renewal. During services one day, he noticed a pile of rubbish stacked in the back of the sanctuary, and asked about it. One of the members laughed:

"Dirt, you say. We have no members, and you worry about a little dirt. Get the members, and we'll clean up the dirt."

Harry said nothing, but appeared the next morning with a mop and a bucket. It was a scorching Sunday in August. The old man carried water and bucket and mop, scrubbed the floor of the 500-seat room and lugged out the waste piles.

He worries about the present. He need only lift his head a little to see the irreversible future: a block away sits the abandoned, torn Netzach Israel Jewish Center and Beth Jacob School for Girls. There, the struggle ended four years ago.

Of the three original Stars of David mounted on stemlike pedestals on the roof of Netzach Israel, only two remain upright. When I was there, a small black boy climbed up on the narrow ledge that held the stars, wrapped his legs around the stem of one of them, sat down and began methodically to rock the star back and forth. He pushed and pulled rhythmically, patiently, for more than half an hour. The thin metal gave slowly at first, then more easily. When the stem finally snapped, and the Star of David, almost as tall as the boy, fell backward into his lap, he scampered up, shrugged it from his legs and ran off, leaving the shiny, broken star   .

He skipped across the roof, grabbed a pipe and slid down to the street. He looked up and smiled cheerfully as I walked over to him. "Why did you break that star?" "Nobody in that building," he replied. "Do you know who was in there?" "Sure. Some kinda church." He raced off, his flashy sneakers kicking through a pile of smashed glass on the front steps.

The building's small, tiled entry foyer was awash in debris. A boy-sized prayer shawl lay on the floor with toilet paper crumbled on top of it. Shredded books covered half the area. One was open to the "Laws of Grace."

A framed photograph of 21 young girls in starched white dresses ("Beth Jacob's First Graduating Class" the legend on it read) was flanked by an opened, but immaculate, beer can and a white skullcap inscribed "Wedding reception, Ruth and Harold Rabinovich, June 9, 1954." A sneaker imprint made the name hard to read.

18

The basement schoolrooms were demolished. The individual wooden desks were topsy-turvy, thrown, ripped. A heavy bookcase had been pulled away from the wall and dumped onto the floor, its contents scattered. Empty beer cans and fragments of small wine bottles intermingled with religious articles of every description. A book of receipts on the floor reported that on January 31, 1961, Mrs. S. Katz had donated $18 to the school. Eighteen in Hebrew means *chay*–life. Through holes in a window, the voices of children, playing happily and talking in Spanish, drifted in.

A stained glass window overlooking the main sanctuary of Netzach Israel had been broken by rocks hurled from the street. It was a memorial window, and enough remained of the hand-painted lettering to read: "In memory of Leib and Dora Phillips–Died November 15, 1924, Died March 19, 1928." I turned and walked out of the building. A man passed as I stood on the steps. "What did you go in there for?" he demanded. "Jews go in there."

Netzach Israel barely achieved its 50th anniversary. Founded in 1908 in a small Bronx store, it moved into its synagogue in 1926. By 1958, the change in the neighborhood had begun to make itself felt. Children pounded on the front door during services. Members were pushed and pelted on the street. The building was broken into so frequently that bars were put on the windows. The synagogue's sisterhood and ladies' auxiliary changed their meetings to the daytime. Evening attendance at services ended. Six years ago, the Beth Jacob School moved. In 1965, the synagogue closed.

The ebb and flow of communities is being repeated in the South Bronx, as elsewhere, perhaps for the final time. The never-ending movement of ethnic groups–Irish, Italians, Jews, Germans–may now, with the coming of the new black and Puerto Rican immigrants, be ending.

The "melting-pot" description given our country (by a foreigner, incidentally) was never more than a pleasant lie. Like clutched to like, and within the cities, ghettos, neighborhoods and communities were born—as isolated, and as fearful, as any in other lands.

In the South Bronx, whites, blacks, Puerto Ricans pass each other and look the other way. There is talk without contact. Substitute Swede for Jew and Slovak for black: the dreadful ballet of separation has not changed.

The story is told in Jewish literature of Rabbi Hillel, sage of the generation before Christ, challenged by an idolator one day to tell him all about Judaism in the brief minutes the questioner could stand on one foot. Hillel replied: "What is hateful to thee, do not do unto thy fellowman. This is the whole law. The rest is mere commentary."

The ethic still eludes men, but the realization that hateful things ultimately become hateful to all parties may be surfacing. And the now-macabre choreography of the slums could be nearing its climactic convulsion. For when the hopeless newcomers, strangers in a sick city and simultaneously aggressors and aggrieved, flail out madly, they either drown or someone must help them.

The latest series of church desecrations in the Bronx (in six months, 68 houses of worship vandalized: 47 Christian churches, 21 synagogues) underscores the isolation of millions in the city. Isolation drives its victims to victimize. The child picked up by the police on his way out of the Intervale synagogue was Puerto Rican. A week later and not too far away, a small race war left two Puerto Ricans and two blacks dead.

A doctor experienced in a South Bronx emergency ward wrote a medical paper and referred almost parenthetically to "one of the bloodiest civilian battlefields of the Northeast." The paper dealt with expedient methods of caring for knife wounds of the chest and abdomen.

The Jews of Intervale are dying. But then, the South Bronx is dying. The anguish of the city misses few. A black mother walks her three children to and from school every day for fear they will otherwise meet a drug addict. Mrs. Perez sends her honor-student son off to fifth grade in the morning and finds him, at lunchtime, dead in an abandoned car behind her home. A departing guardian of the Intervale synagogue, who finally gives up and moves to New Jersey, brings the keys of the building to Harry Kirschner's home and, weeping, pleads: "Please, take care of the *schul*." And Harry Kirschner, a gentle, kind, believing man, scrubs a synagogue and waits for worshipers who will never come back.

END

BOBBY JOINS HIS WORLD

5 MILLION BRAIN-DAMAGED
CHILDREN CAN BE HELPED

THE CHILD IS obviously quick and bright, but he shreds the hearts of his parents. His explosions have pushed him beyond the endurance of his family and his teacher. School routine is impossible when he is in the room. Unable to work at his classmates' first-grade level, he allows no one else to work. Four doctors, one a psychiatrist, have said he is emotionally disturbed, but a year of expensive therapy has not helped. Guilt-ridden and desperate to the point of sleeplessness, his parents are leaning to the advice of one of the physicians who says, "There's nothing more you can do. Put him in a home." They resist. They go to another doctor. Suddenly, the diagnosis changes. The boy's problem is not psychological in origin, but physical. He suffers from an incompletely understood disorganization of the brain that, typically, makes it difficult for him to behave and to learn. The condition most frequently is called minimal brain dysfunction (sometimes, minimal brain damage or learning disabilities). Identified early enough and managed properly, it is usually correctable. Special help is found for the child. Within two years, his gross misbehavior disappears. Under the supervision of teachers at a unique private school, Vanguard in Haverford, Pa., he begins to learn, for the first time, and to grow toward manhood. He is among the few fortunate ones. An estimated five million children in this country, one of every ten school-age youngsters, share his affliction. Remedial facilities in public schools exist for perhaps one percent of them.

Unable to keep pace with his class in public school, he repeated,

21

then dropped out of first grade. His intelligence was "high average," but he never finished his beginning reader. Failure in school pushed him into a shell. The first signs of pressure caused him to fall apart. When he came to Vanguard two years ago, he would not recite in front of his class. A harsh word from a classmate sent him under his desk to sulk. Warmth and special instructions from his teachers, and loving support at home, built a new foundation. During the past year, he has gained two years in reading. His self-confidence now allows him to lead class discussions. He will return to public school next September.

"OUR IGNORANCE IS HUGE. WE GUESS AT CAUSE."

BY CHARLES MANGEL
LOOK Senior Editor

A PSYCHIATRIST WONDERS, "How many kids have we missed? How many sit, at this moment, in homes for the retarded, who are no more retarded than I?"

A worried, angry pediatrician says, "Possibly 75 percent—*three out of four*—of the young men and women who are referred to mental-health centers for psychological help, who drop out of school or become juvenile offenders, had their problems begin with minimal brain dysfunction, and passed through our hands unrecognized.

Minimal brain dysfunction, called by one specialist "the most common neurological problem among children," is in reality a variety of central-nervous-system disruptions. All stem from the brain. All usually affect the child (boys by a margin of at least two-to-one) who has average or better intelligence. All somehow jam up the signals coming into the brain and demanding interpretation and action.

Awareness of this dysfunction is more than two decades old. Researchers explored it before World War II. But, inexplicably and with relatively few exceptions, reports never filtered down to the practicing physicians and the schools, the partnership that must identify and deal with the ailment.

Incredibly, this information still does not reach physicians. Most doctors in practice, experts agree, do not recognize minimal brain dysfunction (a shrinking minority deny its existence). Parents, seeking aid, commonly recite a sad litany of calling upon doctor after doctor to be told, "He is going through a stage; he will grow out of it"; or,

"You have upset him somehow; all of you should go to a psychiatrist"; or, for a child whose worst problem is, say, reading, "Get him a tutor." Now, pushed by parents who have organized as the Association for Children with Learning Disabilities, leaders in medicine, education, child development and public health are beginning to work together.

The task they face is appalling. "Our ignorance of this subject is huge," says Dr. Richard L. Masland, director of the National Institute of Neurological Diseases and Blindness. "We can only guess at cause. We are not dealing with a single condition or disease."

The results of the dysfunction, however, are terrifyingly obvious. The youngster afflicted can have several or most of a group of characteristics. He may find it hard, from the first day of school, to keep up with his class in reading and arithmetic. His spelling may be poor, his penmanship virtually illegible. He may have trouble grasping abstract concepts (are poodles and collies both dogs?) and relating what he has learned in one context to another. His performance may be erratic: high in some areas, low in others.

He may appear to be in perpetual motion, spending more time under his seat than in it. He may be easily distracted, wandering from a teacher in mid-sentence to watch a boy sharpen a pencil. His attention may shift easily, without apparent reason, and his concentration may last only minutes.

Usually, he is emotionally unstable. Moods change from one extreme to another with stunning swiftness. Disappointment, frustration, unexpected variations in simple routine--realities a normal child copes with daily--can cause riotous tantrums, crying spells, hostility or, for some, total withdrawal.

More than three of every four youngsters afflicted appear to be clumsy and awkward. Catching a ball, walking along a chalked line, throwing a beanbag to someone five feet away may be impossible. (A parent says, "I don't care if he never catches a ball." His doctor replies, "If he can't move his hands to the ball, he can't move his hands to reproduce what he sees on the blackboard.")

Researchers think the largest single cause of minimal brain dysfunction is injury during birth. Among other suspected causes: poor prenatal care, oxygen deprivation, illness of the expectant mother, chemical or blood irregularities, genetic inheritance and injuries to the fetus. Severe illness or a blow to the head after birth could have the same result. "In possibly half the instances, we never know the cause," says Dr. Richmond S. Paine, chief of neurology at Children's Hospital, Washington, D.C.

Although symptoms are present during preschool years, the typical youngster does not begin to show severe characteristics until he begins school. Then, pressures begin to build. The young student must now perform certain tasks in specified ways at definite times. Tragically, the vast majority of school systems in the country are not equipped to ferret him out. Hampered by his deficiencies, the minimally brain-damaged youngster gradually falls behind. If his disability doesn't disrupt class routines, he may be allowed to drift, gain "social" promotions and, thus, "graduate." Or, he bides his time, undiscovered and unaided, until he is old enough to leave school and enter an employment market in which he has little chance of success.

If the academic handicaps are severe enough, the youngster may be held back a year or two and eventually be assigned to a catch-all class with others who have learning problems—slow learners, the mentally retarded or the disturbed. He may receive psychological counseling. Remedial experts may try to help with specific academic problems. Each will fail because the basic underlying problem remains undetected.

During the period of academic failure, the youngster begins to learn about social rejection. Inept in play, he is soon abandoned by classmates. Adults, judging his emotional cartwheels, dismiss him as spoiled or, worse, disturbed. Aware of his failures, the youngster becomes frustrated, assumes he is worthless and gives up on himself and school. Now, true psychological problems begin, triggered by a total inability to succeed in anything.

The agony is unnecessary. "We still do not know enough to identify all children who suffer from minimal brain dysfunction," says Dr. Leon Eisenberg, professor of child psychiatry at Johns Hopkins University School of Medicine in Baltimore. "There are no precise, yes-no, tests. But by a combination of means, a group of qualified examiners can find most of these children."

Experts recommend a team examination of children suspected of having the dysfunction. The group should consist of a psychologist, neurologist, pediatrician and an educator trained to recognize and treat the ailment. A psychiatrist and hearing and speech therapists may join the group.

If the diagnosis is positive, education (either in the form of special classes or tutorial assistance) becomes the key to improvement. "These are intellectually competent youngsters," says Dr. Milton Brutten, psychologist and clinical director of The Vanguard School. "Many range high into the gifted category. They can learn and overcome much or all of their disabilities with skill and compassion on our part."

Vanguard designs special classes to meet the individual needs of these students. Each teacher has six to ten pupils. Rooms are small, to lessen the temptation of the hyperactive child to roam. Distractions are minimized. Floors are carpeted to decrease noise. Movable desks allow a child who wants to be alone to turn to the wall.

But the decisive element is the teacher. Not only must she be willing to work patiently with a child likely to burst into song during an arithmetic lesson, she must also be able to understand and deal with the underlying causes of the learning problems. Does one of her students have difficulty interpreting the symbols we call the alphabet? She must be able to devise special techniques to fill in gaps in the child's learning process. Where required, remedial specialists supplement classroom efforts. Drugs may be useful in calming a child and helping him to concentrate on school work.

The fearful term, brain damage, surprisingly reassures parents, once their doctor tells them the condition is physical, not psychological, and can be dealt with. Parental help is essential. Now aware that their child's inability in school is not a result of stupidity, and his behavior not willful, they give him the support any youngster needs. Consistent rules control his behavior; discipline is fair but firm. Situations likely to stimulate him excessively, such as a long shopping spree, are avoided. He gets ample time for discharge of overabundant energy. Family activities are as simple as possible.

The growth of Vanguard, and of a small but growing number

of schools like it, indicates the compelling need for special-education facilities. Founded as an 11-month day school in 1960 by Dr. Brutten and teacher-administrator Henry D. Evans, Vanguard has leaped from four students to 365, in spite of a $3,000 annual fee. A boarding branch opened this year in Lake Wales, Fla.

The failure to provide special education for children with minimal cerebral dysfunction constitutes what a doctor in the Public Health Service terms "a major national problem." The Office of Education estimates that more than 60,000 specialist teachers are needed. There are perhaps 2,000. Fifteen states offer "some" assistance; few of them claim they are even beginning to meet the need.

"These children are on a precipice," says Evans, Vanguard's educational director. "They cannot fit in a regular program. They will deteriorate if they are thrust, willy-nilly, into one of the traditional 'special' classes for the handicapped. If we can catch them early enough, ideally when they start school, and teach them properly, most will become self-sufficient. But as of this moment, too many are being lost."

END

THE TRAGEDY AND HOPE OF
RETARDED CHILDREN

BY DR. BURTON BLATT with CHARLES MANGEL
Chairman, Department of Special Education
Boston University

You SEE the children first. An anonymous boy, about six, squeezes his hand through the opening at the bottom of a locked door and begs, "Touch me. Play with me." A 13-year-old boy lies naked, on his own wastes, in a corner of a solitary-confinement cell. Children, one and two years old, lie silent in cribs all day, without contact with any adult, without playthings, without any apparent stimulation. The cribs are placed side by side and head to head to fill every available bit of space in the room.

I have recently seen these children in the back wards of four Eastern state-supported institutions for the mentally retarded. Although I had visited these "homes" before—and scores of others like them during my 18 years as a member of long-forgotten advisory panels—I had paid little attention to their back areas. (Several colleagues arranged my tour through the places few but selected staff personnel ever see.)

Now I know what people mean when they say there is a hell on earth.

The institutions I visited, located in three different states, are huge repositories for human beings. The largest contains some 6,000 adults and children. The smallest, about 1,000 of all ages. It is the sight of the children that tears at you.

Each of the dormitories for the severely retarded had what some like to call a recreation, or day, room. Groups of young children occupied them, lying on the floor, rocking, sitting, sleeping—alone. An attendant, silently watching, was the only adult in many of these rooms. Some had no adults at all.

The six-year-old who begged, "Touch me," was one of 40 or more unkempt children of various ages crawling around a bare floor in a bare room. Their dormitory held about 100 children. It was connected to nine other dormitories containing 900 more.

In one dayroom, two male attendants stood by as half a dozen fights flared in different corners of the room. Three teen-agers were silently punching each other near a barred window. One young child, about five, was biting a second boy. Another resident, about 20, had backed a boy of about 10 into a far corner and was kicking him viciously, every now and then looking back at us. There were about 50 persons in the room. Their ages ranged from about 5 to 80.

Some dormitories had solitary-confinement cells. Attendants called them "therapeutic isolation." They were solitary confinement in the most punitive and inhumane form.

These cells were generally tiny rooms, approximately 7'x7', shielded by locked, heavy doors. A small opening, covered by bars or a closely-meshed screen, allowed observation.

Some cells had mattresses, some blankets, some nothing but the bare floor. None that I saw, and I examined these cells in every institution I visited, had either a bed, a washstand or a toilet.

I found the naked, 13-year-old boy in one of these cells. He had been in confinement for several days because he had cursed an attendant. A younger child, at another institution, had been put into solitary confinement for five days because he had broken several windows.

I asked the attendant in charge of one dormitory what he needed most to supervise residents better and to provide them with a more adequate program. His answer: The addition of two more cells.

(These solitary cells are usually on an upper floor, away from the scrutiny of official visitors. A commissioner of mental health in a western state, who had heard I was preparing this story for LOOK, called to ask if these conditions existed in his state's institutions. He is the chief mental-health official in his state.)

Children are tied down. I saw many whose hands or legs were

bound or waists secured. (One boy, tied on the floor to a bench leg, was trying to roll away from a pool of urine. He could not.) The terribly undermanned staffs used binds as their ultimate resort. The attendant who asked for two new solitary-confinement cells was, with one assistant, responsible for an entire multilevel dormitory housing 100 severely retarded residents.

Almost in desperation, he asked me, "What can we do with those patients who do not conform? We must lock them up or restrain them or sedate them or put fear into them."

I felt at that moment much the same as men of conscience felt, I imagine, upon reading Dr. Johann Christian Reil's description of institutional problems. "We lock these unfortunate creatures in lunatic cells, as if they were criminals," that physician said. "We keep them in chains in forlorn jails ... where no sympathetic human being can ever bestow on them a friendly glance, and we let them rot in their own filth." This, in 1803.

Every room in the living quarters of young children—and the moderately and severely retarded of any age—had a stout door and locks. Attendants routinely passed from room to room with a key chain in hand, locking and unlocking as they went.

Some of the children's dormitories offered "nursery programs." These were few and primitive. Several children in one of the "nursery" rooms had severe lacerations from banging their heads against walls and floors. When confronted with young, severely retarded children, many professionals believe head-banging inevitable. This is arrogant nonsense. Head-banging can be drastically reduced in an environment where children are not ignored.

Adults in these institutions fared no better than the children. Many of their dayrooms had a series of bleacherlike benches. Residents sat on them all day, often naked, jammed together, without purposeful activity or any kind of communication with each other. Countless human beings on rows and rows of benches in silent rooms, waiting for—what? One or two attendants stood in each room. Their main function was to hose down the floor periodically to drive wastes into a sewer drain.

Although men and women were kept in separate dayrooms, the

scenes in each were the same. The odor was overpowering. Excrement was seemingly everywhere, on walls, ceilings. The smell was permanent and ghastly. I could not endure more than a few minutes in each room.

The physical facilities contributed to the visual horror. All of the quarters were gloomy, barren. Even the television sets in several of the dayrooms appeared to be co-conspirators in gloom: they were broken. (The residents, however, continued to sit on their benches, in neat rows, looking at the blank tubes.)

I heard a good deal of laughter, but there was little cheer. Adult residents played ring-around-a-rosy. Other adults, in the vocational-training center, were playing jacks. Although they were not always the severely retarded, this was the only way they were allowed to behave.

I was told, during one visit, about the development of a new research center. The assistant superintendent said "materials" would come from the institution, and the center would need about 30 or 40 "items."

I didn't know what he meant. After some mumbling, I finally understood. At that institution, and apparently at others in that state, patients are called "materials" and personnel, "items."

It was so difficult not to believe that this man was joking that, during later visits to other dormitories in that institution, I asked the attending physicians, "How many 'items' have you in this building? How much 'material' do you have?" Each man knew exactly what I was asking.

Each of the institutions was incredibly overcrowded. The one housing 6,000 had been built for 4,000. Beds were jammed so tightly together that it was impossible in some dormitories to cross parts of the rooms without walking on the beds. The beds were often without pillows. I saw mattresses so sagged by years and the weight of countless bodies that they scraped the floor.

Signs of gross neglect pockmarked many of the older buildings. I saw gaping holes in the ceilings of such vital areas as a main kitchen; in toilets, urinals were ripped out, sinks broken, bowls backed up.

I will not reveal the names of these four institutions. First, it would lead to the inevitable dismissal of the men who arranged our visit. They want conditions altered as badly as we do. Second, I don't want anyone to think that we are discussing just these four "homes." They are the symbol of a national disgrace. *These four institutions represent the current conditions in portions of the majority of state-supported institutions for the retarded in this country.* This story arose in the hope that attention directed to the desperate needs of these institutions would help open the way to improving them.

Tax-supported institutions for retarded children and adults do not have to be like this. We know better. We can do better–if we want to. A pleasant, estate-like home and school, the Seaside Regional Center in Waterford, Conn., has shown us how.

Seaside resembles a private, and expensive, school. It explodes with noise, the healthful noise of activity, and with color–walls, draperies, decorations, wherever children are. It also explodes with the pride a person takes in doing an important job better than most.

Tim was one of Seaside's youngest admissions. Uncontrollable at home, he had been placed in another institution two years earlier. He was four when he reached Seaside, and helpless. He lay in bed all day. He could not walk or talk. He was totally unaware of anything occurring about him. His label from the earlier institution: severely retarded.

He began to get individual attention. He was taught to dress, to eat, to go to the bathroom. Slowly, words came and then steps. He was put into a preschool class at Seaside. Six months later, he joined a preschool class with children of average intelligence in Waterford. Last fall, he entered kindergarten, and 11 months ago, went home. He is now in first grade in his home community. His IQ, which leaped dramatically before he left Seaside, may yet move into the average range.

Chester, 12 when he came to Seaside, had already spent four years in another institution. He could barely talk. He trembled when anyone approached him. In 12 months, he was discharged. His IQ had risen almost one-third. He is now in public school for the first time.

A mother writes a note to Seaside superintendent Fred Finn: "[After] a year ... it almost seems like [our son's] rebirth." Another parent adds, "Betsy entered Seaside a year ago.... There had been much newspaper publicity about the terrible conditions in some state institutions for the … retarded. Seaside is the living proof that it doesn't have to be this way. My husband and I drove up to look the school over for the first time with a considerable amount of apprehension…. To our amazement, instead of shock and sadness, the strongest emotion in our hearts on our drive back was a feeling of joy…. This was … a big, loving home…. [Betsy would not be] a number, but a very special person…. If I were to talk to parents who have just learned that they have a retarded child, I would tell them two things. First, don't be afraid to love and to get to know your child, no matter who advises you to the contrary. Second, don't be afraid to investigate your state institutions. You may be pleasantly surprised as we were. If you aren't, join those who are trying to do something about it. It can be done."

Each of these children came to Seaside from other state institutions diagnosed as custodial cases. Each could have been groveling in the back wards of the four institutions we visited, had they been there.

Seaside is a clear break with the past. Opened six years ago as an experiment, it is a small, state-supported regional center designed to be a clearinghouse for all problems involving retardation within a two-county area. It was the nation's first. It has been so successful that Connecticut has already approved 11 more like it.

Two hundred and forty men, women and children of all ability levels live at Seaside, a 36-acre complex of grassy areas, buildings and woods on the shore of Long Island Sound. Everyone works at something, every day.

One hundred and sixty children attend school, half in the Waterford system and the rest in classes of five or six at Seaside. Forty, the most severely retarded, have daily activity and self-help programs. Forty young adults are getting job training. Some will move into the community and become self-supporting with little or no supervision. Others will stay at Seaside as paid, part-time employees.

Seaside reaches out. The panic that can crush a family unable to cope alone with a retarded child is relieved by the safety-valve role Seaside plays. Half of its programs are in the community. The center helps 850 non-resident retarded children or adults and their families.

It operates recreation programs in seven communities, day-care centers in five (for children able to live at home, but not eligible for school), two sheltered workshops and two day camps. There is no waiting list. No one is ignored.

Seaside, for the first time in this nation's history, has given parents alternatives to keeping an unmanageable child at home without anyone to turn to (more than half the nation's school districts have no classes for the retarded), or putting him into the usual institution, often for life.

Relatively few children must be placed in an institution. Most parents, in these cases, want to stay close to their children and to take them home as soon as possible. Too many institutions have built-in systems to separate a child from his family. Some, organized for the convenience of the staff, operate like prisons. When parents visit, for example, their child is brought to, and taken from, a common visiting room.

At Seaside, parents are virtually everywhere. They have no special hours or off-limit areas. They can come when they like, make special trips to feed a youngster if they want. Seaside will take in a child for a month to give a harassed mother a chance to rest, or for a week if parents want to take a vacation trip.

This takes money. Seaside costs more than the typical institution. Nationally, the average cost in institutions for the retarded is less than $5 per day for each patient. Six states spend less than $2.50. Only seven spend more than $5.50.

The federal prison system spends $7.67 daily to maintain each inmate. Our better zoos average $7 a day for the care and feeding of some of their larger animals.

Seaside spends $12 a day for each resident. In terms of human suffering and the potential for human growth, places like Seaside are among the few really economical, government-sponsored institutions I know.

Our nation's "homes" for the retarded contain thousands of Timmys and Chesters. Almost 200,000 persons are now in them. About 50 percent are under 20.

Conservatively, at least half of these young people could live and work in their communities if they were properly taught and if supervision were available. We spend about $200,000 to support one person for his lifetime in a state institution for the retarded.

Seaside discharged 40 percent of its residents last year, about eight times the national average. Children went home and into public school, able to live within–not destroy–their families. Adults got jobs.

Seaside is proving that retardation is not unalterable. The capacity of a retarded person can be changed, up or down, within limits, depending upon the way he is treated. Most retarded youngsters can be taught to support themselves. Intelligence is influenced by practice and training, just as it is enhanced, or limited, by inheritance, injury or environment.

Seaside wages a strong fight against inertia. Its staff has scant patience for tomorrow, for in a few short tomorrows, children become adults, and residents potentially able to develop can be transformed into stagnant inmates.

"We have no magic," says Superintendent Fred Finn. "We just do not believe that because a child hasn't, means that he can't. The children who have made remarkable progress ... at Seaside after years of institutionalization [elsewhere] obviously had this potential, but ... it was not developed. I challenge every family..., if it is dissatisfied with conditions..., to protest immediately. Each of these children is entitled to the best and the most any child gets. If one of them can do nothing more than creep, then he will learn to creep."

Teaching a retarded child with an IQ of perhaps 30, and a severe emotional problem, is like teaching no other youngster. You have to want to teach him. Then you have to fight with him for each micro-inch of progress. When you win a little, you glow. I had lunch one day recently in Seaside's dining hall with two teachers who were gloating because one seven-year-old charge had just, that morning, uttered his first comprehensible, one-syllable word.

A special love exists at Seaside, a love capable of belief in the fulfillment of another human being. I am exasperated with institutional staffs that have offered me excuses, rationalizations and explanations for their behavior. Although I am not unsympathetic about their inadequate budgets, over-crowded dormitories–leading to the concessions they make and the programs they conduct—their actions speak primarily of their character.

Mental retardation can bring out the best in healthy people as well as the worst. The retarded will not get the care and education they deserve until institutions cause those who minister to their needs to become more rather than less sensitive.

Some human beings have been taught to conceive of others as they think of animals. It isn't that some attendants are cruel—although, too often, they are—but that they have come to believe that those in their charge are not really human.

When one views a group of human beings as "material," an increased budget for resident care and additional staff alone could never cause the radical changes necessary in institutional treatment. The use of such terms demonstrates the basic problem that has to be solved before state institutions for the retarded will alter substantially: We must become more optimistic concerning human behavior and its ability to change.

William James wrote, "The greatest discovery of my generation is that human beings can alter their lives by altering their attitudes of mind." The belief that intelligence is educable refers both to children and those who must deal professionally with them. For Helen Keller to have changed as she did, Anne Sullivan also had to. For children in back wards to change, their attendants must, too. To the extent we can influence the latter's concept of human potential, we shall influence the former's educability.

Every institution, including those discussed earlier in this article, has superb, dedicated attendants and professional staffs. Yet for so many of their residents, they could not possibly do any less than they now do. It is irrelevant how well the rest of an institution's program is being handled if these back wards exist. We have got to instill a fundamental belief among all who work with the retarded that each of them is equally human, not equally intellectually able, not equally physically appealing, but sharing a common humanity.

What can we do? We must at least double per capita expenditures in state institutions and reduce the size of these institutions. In addition:

1. In each state, a board of impartial institutional visitors should be appointed by the governor. This board would report directly to the highest state officials. Appointments should be without regard to political affiliation. They should be based on both knowledge of human welfare and demonstrated public service.

2. Within each state institution for the retarded, the staff of each department (e.g., medical, educational) should have its own board of advisers. This board, through regular visits, would know the institution's problems. Its members could become involved without endangering employees who trust them, because the board would not be responsible for ratings, raises or promotions. Problems now hidden could be given the exposure necessary for solutions.

3. In each state, one university should be given responsibility and resources to provide adequate refresher training and counsel to all institutional employees, from chief administrative officers to rawest attendant recruits.

4. In each state, at least one institution for the retarded should become a center for compulsory, periodic retraining of everyone employed by the state to work with the retarded. Each new employee should have to spend a specified period in the training center.

Few institutions for the retarded in this country are completely free of dirt, odors, naked patients, children in locked cells, horribly crowded dormitories and understaffed and wrongly-staffed facilities. Countless people are suffering needlessly at this moment. The families of these victims of our irresponsibility are in anguish, for they know, or suspect, the truth. Unwittingly, or unwillingly, they have been forced to institutionalize their loved ones into lives of degradation and horror.

I hold responsible each superintendent, each commissioner of mental health, each governor—ultimately, each thoughtful citizen—for the care and treatment of individuals committed to institutions in their state. I challenge every institution in the U.S. to look at itself—to justify its programs, admission policies, personnel, budgets, philosophy.

I challenge every family of a resident in a state institution for the retarded, if it is dissatisfied with conditions at that institution, to protest immediately and repetitively to the governor and to join with other families to force legislative action.

The President's Committee on Mental Retardation reported in August: "Three-quarters of the nation's ... institutionalized mentally retarded live in buildings 50 years old or more." It demanded the virtual doubling of the full-time staff in these institutions "to reach *minimum adequacy*." Among its conclusions: "Many [facilities and programs] are a disgrace to the nation and to the states that operate them."

We must have a national examination that will inspect the deepest recess of the most obscure back ward in the least progressive state. A national, qualified commission with authority should review state budgets for the care and treatment of the retarded. Sincere state officials will leap to cooperate.

I will be surprised if this article will change the nature of state institutions for the retarded. My current depression will not permit such grand thoughts. But, as Albert Camus wrote: "Perhaps we can't stop the world from being one in which children are tortured, but we can reduce the number of tortured children."

END

A CHILD HAS TO BE TRAINED TO LOVE

By Charles Mangel
LOOK Senior Editor

A CHILD'S FIRST YEARS are his most important. During this period, character is formed, intelligence is most malleable. The two vital ingredients: the love and stability provided by parents.

For a rapidly growing army of Americans –300,000 at best estimate– the vital ingredients are missing. These are the kids novelist Pearl Buck calls "the lost children," those without functioning parents, who spend at least part of their lives in foster homes or institutions.

The ultimate victims, chiefly of extramarital sex (source of 80 percent of all cases), family discord and trouble, uncountable thousands of them are destined to live without families until they are 18. Then they're on their own.

The problem is frightening. The national inability to deal with it may be worse.

"We know that a great many of these youngsters—perhaps most— will have personality disorders throughout their lives," says a child psychologist. "They will find their way into our prisons and our mental hospitals. They will find it extremely difficult to adjust to people, to make a good marital and family adjustment of their own." (Half of all children over 12 who are picked for adoption are later rejected. They are so beaten down, they can't make it in a family.)

"Yet," he adds, "we see no sort of comprehensive effort being made to find an answer. Incredibly, we even see some adoption-agency people, the professionals concerned with the problem, still thinking as they did 20 years ago."

There has been progress. Pressed by the growing number of children thrust upon them, public and private adoption agencies have made adoption far easier for qualified people. It has never been as easy as it is right now, in most areas of the nation, to adopt children.

Adoptions have increased almost two-thirds over the past decade to 152,000 children annually. But illegitimacy has tripled since 1940. The record for the latest year: 302,400 births out of wedlock.

About 15 years ago, virtually the only child who could be placed with adoptive parents was white and in perfect health. Today, many of the barriers have eased, both for children who need adoption and adults who want to adopt.

Men and women seeking adoption once had to be under 43 and 38, respectively. Couples in their 50's can now adopt.

Applicants for children once had to prove infertility as a matter of course. More and more adoption workers now rebel against what they term a "degrading" invasion of privacy.

Prospective adoptive parents traditionally had to be married at least three years before they could ask for a child. Many agencies now require only one year.

Children used to be rationed to adoptive parents with two as a common limit. In some areas of the country, the right couple today can adopt as many as six, even ten, children.

Adults once had to be in perfect health themselves. Recently, a family headed by a paraplegic adopted a child. Children no longer have to be perfect. A blind child has been adopted in California.

Some families once waited up to five years for a child. Many now wait less than six months.

Yet all this is not enough. New ideas are needed; some are coming, but slowly. An exchange organization has begun to match children and parents who live in different areas of this country and Canada. (A forerunner group successfully placed 300 Indian children in non-Indian homes.)

New York state and California are experimenting with small subsidies for adoptive parents who need financial help.

Among the latest concepts is the adoption of children by unmarried adults.

Although some children had been taken before into homes with only one adult, the cases were rare. Usually, the adopting adult was a member of the child's original family.

The Los Angeles County Department of Adoptions, largest in the country, three years ago began the first large-scale attempt to provide children with single parents. What started as an experiment within a year gained formal approval.

The program is designed for children generally ignored by two-parent applicants: the racially mixed youngster, the child with a physical handicap.

Los Angeles' problems are typical. Although the county finds homes for an estimated 2,500 children a year, it has a waiting list of two-parent homes for the "preferred" children: 175 couples hoping for healthy, white infants.

Waiting, too, are 341 hard-to-place children, chiefly, 222 black and 75 who are white and need medical treatment.

Single adults have adopted 59 children in Los Angeles since the new program began. One woman, a high school math teacher, has already come back for a second child. Forty-one of the youngsters are black; ten have mixed ancestry, mainly Mexican-American; and seven are white with varying kinds of medical problems. Thirteen of the adoptions cross racial lines. In each case, a white woman took a racially mixed child. All but one of the new parents are women. Only two of the trials have failed.

"The program has worked beyond expectation," says Walter A. Heath, director of the Los Angeles department. "We went into it with our fingers crossed, expecting at best to place a few children whom no one else would take. Now, we believe we are just getting started. We can do much more, and we intend to."

The 59 children now in permanent homes underline the merit of the single-parent approach. "Beyond question, the future of these children would have been a changing series of foster homes," says Heath. "A few might have been lucky enough to get long-term foster parents. I strongly doubt if more than several would have found two-parent homes."

The value to the new parents was unplanned. Mrs. Carol Coria, at

31 the youngest to adopt a child, had wanted a large family. Then her husband died after a long illness, and she "just stopped feeling." It took three years and a five-month-old, half-Asian girl, whom she named Amie, to return her "to a sense of love and a desire, basically, to live again."

Bright, attractive, Mrs. Coria speaks articulately of what Amie has meant to her: "I had become so ingrown in the years after my husband died that when Amie came, I could not adjust to the change in myself. The first month, I found it hard to recognize myself in the mirror. It seemed as if someone else were there staring at me, someone quite a bit better. I felt old when I took Amie. Now, I have never felt as young."

Clara McGinty adopted an infant at 52. A gregarious, friendly schoolteacher, she holds John David (part-Caucasian, part-Indian) on her lap, lets him tug at her short-cropped gray hair and laughs about "getting into the diaper business at a grandmother's age."

She, too, talks about the benefit to both of them: "I have had so many blessings in health, work, family and friends that I wanted to share my life with someone else. John David has just delighted me, although it has been much harder than I had imagined (walking the floor at my age)." Migraine headaches have lessened considerably, as well as "a certain bitchiness I had before John David moved in."

Although a demonstrated success in Los Angeles, and in spite of extreme interest by adoption agencies throughout the country, the single-parent idea has yet to get the broad approval necessary if it is to do much good. Only eight states and the District of Columbia have tried it (although it is possible in all states). An estimated 200 children have been placed.

Probably the greatest barrier still standing is the reluctance of a number of adoption officials to accept it. "Any innovative idea is slow to start," says Myron R. Chevlin, an assistant executive director of the Child Welfare League of America. "Some adoption people want two parents or none. They are waiting for the millennium."

"All of us in this business must face up to the fact that the rule of two parents for every child just cannot apply to all children," says Los Angeles' Heath. "We must find a number of new alternatives. Single-parent adoption is one."

Heath, an intensely compassionate man, worries about children without homes they can call their own. "A child has to be trained over a period of years to be a member of a family, to love," he says. "If he has never received, how can we expect him to give?"

It is long past the time, writes Pearl Buck, an adoptive parent herself, when "we must consider the nature of love, how to give it, how to receive it. It is the loveless man and woman who threaten our national life and culture."

END

THE REMARKABLE MR. HARRIS

By Charles Mangel
LOOK Senior Editor

It was summer on the old plantation. Blistering hot. Dust swirling. Ants in the drinking water. The hands were crawling down the cotton rows, grabbing the bolls and throwing them into the sacks they dragged behind them. Fred Harris, 12, stood suddenly, looked heavenward and pleaded, "Lord, get me *outa* here."

Undeniably, heaven has responded. Harris, 38, now finds himself working the political rows in Washington. He is no longer on his knees. There are a few other differences.

The Democratic party today is a curious, headless affair. The boss is gone, and the jousting is proceeding briskly. Humphrey was defeated, "but don't count me out." Ted Kennedy gambled, won the post of Senate Democratic whip in January and set out for the presidency. Muskie, suddenly a celebrity, is off addressing the nation. One more principal must be added: Harris, just four years out of Oklahoma obscurity and, possibly, the most remarkable of the four.

A state senator who had been elected to fill the unexpired term of the late Robert S. Kerr, Harris entered the capital totally without notice in 1964. Hardworking, hobbyless, he proceeded to compile an upswing record. Within nine months, he had a subcommittee to chair, a feat very few first-year men have accomplished. In a bit more than two years, he added a seat on the finance committee, a major Senate unit. *That* doesn't hardly happen.

He quickly established a broad-gauged interest, primarily in human needs. He fought, along with Bob Kennedy, for a range of improvements in the welfare system and to increase job opportunities for the poor and the unskilled. He introduced a bill, still stymied, to create a National Foundation for the Social Sciences, to provide them with the kind of attention and visibility that the National Science Foundation gives to the natural sciences. He joined Senator Walter Mondale of Minnesota to sponsor legislation that would create a President's Council of Social Advisors. The council, still a paper dream, would attempt to set national social priorities, balance federal spending for schools against, say, the space effort, and to measure the nation's social advances. No one, Harris and Mondale insist, is doing this systematic weighing and sifting now.

During the Detroit riot of July 1967, Harris proposed a commission to investigate racial disorders. President Johnson quickly created the National Advisory Commission on Civil Disorders and named Harris one of the 11 members. Harris soon asserted the force of leadership that trademarks him. Some former staff members of that panel now suggest he was its most valuable addition, both in helping to keep the members of the group talking to each other and in helping to persuade them to agree unanimously on the essence of the black-white problem: separate societies created and maintained, however unconsciously, by the larger one. Anything less than *full* discussion of the problem would be shameless caviling, Harris argued over and over.

The commission's work brought Harris his first measure of national awareness. The study sold a million copies, but has been ignored by the bulk of the country. (Do you know anyone who has read it?) He remained little known.

When Humphrey named Harris and Mondale to lead his pre-convention campaign, the pair were dismissed by many as "brass Boy Scouts." As late as last July, with the word out that Humphrey, the favorite for the Democratic nomination, was seriously considering Harris as his running mate, people still were able to ask, "Fred who?" Ditto last January, when Humphrey did ask the Democratic National Committee to elect Harris chairman. Even awareness that Harris almost ran with Humphrey (it was Muskie and Harris in separate bedrooms as Humphrey paced his Conrad Hilton suite, and the decision was about as close as it could have gotten) did not markedly improve public recognition of the Oklahoma Senator.

Harris finally is surfacing–in part because of the Democratic National Committee chairmanship, but more because of the cumulative effect of an extraordinary capacity for work, a quickness of mind and a personal charm that have won for him good friends in conservative and liberal segments of both parties. I asked Humphrey, a 16-year veteran of the Senate, to characterize Harris's rise there. The former vice president didn't try to hedge: "I don't know of any man who has come along faster."

Born to the kind of rural poverty that forces a four-year-old to work in the fields with his entire family, Harris has a clear link to the poor and minorities he speaks for in the Senate. His parents, neither of whom reached high school (he is the only one in his family to get to college), worked at many things, including, in Harris's early years, migrant farming. "We lived in garages and empty old houses," a sister recalls, "and brought our things in boxes." Harris knows the bite of prejudice, too, in part from his wife LaDonna, who is half-Comanche. Indians in the Southwest don't fare that much better than black. The word is gut-eater in place of nigger or kike.

Fred and LaDonna, who is three months younger, met in Walters (Okla.) High School. They married during Fred's freshman year at the University of Oklahoma. Both went to work at the university fulltime, while Fred also studied. Sweat and scholarships paid the bills. Fred won election to Phi Beta Kappa and paced his law-school class each year.

I met Harris in the fall of 1966 when I was researching a story about LaDonna and her work as founder of an Indian self-help organization back home. It was during Harris's campaign for reelection, and we talked for the first time aboard a train hired by a group of candidates to whistlestop a day's worth of small rural communities. I asked Harris why he wanted to be in the Senate.

Slumped on a folding chair, shoes off, tie askew and cigarette ashes dribbling down his shirt front, Harris replied, "In essence, because I want to help form the issues that will shape my life." Okay, but fairly routine, I thought then. Yet Harris has apparently meant what he said. For example, the riot-study group targeted three main areas as the key problems: racism, poverty, powerlessness; the last being the inability of most (of whatever age, color, money) to influence the things that push and pull at us. Of the ten men and a woman on that commission, Harris has been the only one (with the exception of Mayor Lindsay of New York) to continue to bear down on those problems. For him, the riot study was a beginning, not an end.

In his book *Alarms and Hopes*, published last year, he said about racism: "Many ... who have either approved of or acquiesced in discrimination against the black have thereby, consciously or unconsciously, denied ... the inborn dignity and worth of every human soul.... As a nation, we have been living a false life, and, deep down, we know it and have known it all along."

Addressing himself to all the poor, not solely the black, he moved in on the cliché query: Do poor people, on welfare, really want to work? "I think it is gravely wrong to think that, somehow, poor people are not like the rest of us. We say to ourselves that we know we would not want to be ... on welfare. We know we would rather be self-sufficient and self-respecting, but for some reason we think most poor people would not. I [don't] believe that is ... true."

Harris speaks frequently of the effects of powerlessness, and resulting alienation. He told a Washington luncheon group last year, "Each of us must say to ourselves, every now and then, 'What am I really doing with my life? What am I really doing that makes any difference to anybody? Where is the value and the worth in my life or, for that matter, in society?' Psychoanalyst Erich Fromm has said that the deepest need of man is 'to overcome his separateness, to leave the prison of his aloneness.' We must, somehow, find a way in which all of us can again feel that we are participating in our country, have some control over the pattern of our lives."

Not a spellbinder, Harris talks with a compelling sense of urgency. He is direct. To a group of wealthy women in New York, he said recently, "Before you criticize a welfare mother, I suggest you go and visit one." To a Peace Corps trainee who complained, "I'm sick of Vietnam," he replied, "I am too. I'm also sick of malnutrition in Mississippi." To Chamber of Commerce types in Little Rock, he was loud and clear, "I received a call asking if I could help a black air force major who had just returned [to his Southern home] from Vietnam and whose son had died and couldn't be buried in the local cemetery. It is too late for that in America. It is just too late for that." The clarity is stark.

Novelist George Orwell once worried about the inability of intellectuals "to see that human society must be based on common decency, whatever the political and economic forms ...." Harris, an intellectual by any definition, appears unlikely to forget these needs. An Indian social worker who had worked with him told me, "He excites you because he cares. He touches your life."

In a time when politicians bore us more than ever (at least it seems that way to me), Harris challenges people. Lacking the glitter of a Kennedy or a Lindsay, he has an infecting earnestness. A young, prosperous Oklahoma City dentist told me, "My wife and I had never paid much attention to politics until we heard Fred speak, and later met him. He made us think, then work. For the first time, I am now digging into my own community. I never knew a black man until I was in college. Yet now I have read, and support, every word of the civil-disorders report."

A black businessman in Lawton, Okla., where Harris practiced law until 1964, is emphatic about him. "Fred and LaDonna were among the first white people to join with us when we decided it was time to integrate Lawton's public facilities. LaDonna picketed with us. We trust these two." At the crest of Senator McCarthy's presidential drive, Harris–linked to Humphrey, and thus, nominally, to Johnson–visited a Peace Corps training center. He listened to a group of young men serenade with a carefully rehearsed "Gene, Gene, he's so clean." Then Harris began to talk quietly about what he had learned as he prowled America's cities researching the civil-disorder report. The formal program ended, but the young people kept him there, talking into the night.

Harris's great strength, perhaps his greatest, is his ability to understand and work with opposing factions. Although he opposed Medicare in 1965 (he now says he was wrong), he is considered a ranking liberal. In the intensely personal and subtle society of the

Senate, he was able to make an unsuccessfulx try for the number three party job, conference secretary, in 1967, opposing Russell Long's choice, Sen. Robert C. Byrd, of W. Va., yet keep Long as a friend. In a town that gingerly balanced the Johnson-Humphrey and the Bob Kennedy forces, he was close to both, socially close to Bob and Ethel and Hubert and Muriel, politically close to Johnson. Such disparate souls as John Gardner, former Secretary of HEW and now chairman of the Urban Coalition, and Mississippi Senator James Eastland agree, in almost the identical words, that "Harris will become a leader."

But back home in Oklahoma, Harris's work with the riot commission may be costing him votes. A political writer there says, "He is way ahead of us. He may be more than Oklahoma deserves. But I don't know if Fred could win an election here now, or in '72 when his term expires."

Harris appears relatively untroubled by these reports: "Issues like this are too basic to compromise. If I didn't want to deal with them, I wouldn't have come to the Senate. But, you know, if you ever get away from what you think is right, you are in terrible trouble. You won't know what you stand for, and you won't be able to defend yourself."

He has led his constituency before. The noisiest effort, in Oklahoma, almost cost him his Senate seat there. Harris and three other state senators proposed, against vast opposition, a transfer of roads from the jurisdiction of locally elected county commissioners to the state highway department. Under the commissioners, road operation was inefficient. Waste, presumably graft, piled high. The proposal was murdered in the state Senate, and Harris thought his political death would come in the next election.

Yet he won, although his three co-sponsors were defeated. He remained in the Oklahoma Senate long enough to see much of his program adopted, largely by administrative procedure, and it brought a far more efficient road system to the state.

"You just never know," he says now. "I was absolutely convinced, after we lost that attempt, that they were going to wind up by beating me. I think I realized then the right thing usually turns out to be the best thing. I have a lot of faith in people. If you can let them see the problems through your eyes, you can usually convince a majority of them that you've come to the right view."

Talking some months ago of the failure of Lyndon Johnson to support the riot-study findings, Harris said quietly, "You know, Teddy Roosevelt called the presidency a bully pulpit. He was right. There is no other force anywhere quite like it."

Harris has inherited the Democratic party at conceivably its lowest point in a generation. Once-traditional voting segments are drifting, or being torn, away. He has promised to use the committee, in concert with Congressional leaders, to speak for the party while it is out of the White House, to help it find again a solid base of popular support: "We can't simply oppose; we must develop our own program, propose our own alternatives." It is easy to see Harris leading the Democrats, now and later.

END

WARPAINT FOR THE SENATOR'S WIFE

No ROAD EXISTS. You teeter across a stream, bend under two low white birches and you see the shack. Seven people call it home. It has two rooms, open holes for windows, no doors. It has no water, no electricity. The bathroom is that clump of bushes 20 yards from the entrance. Four calendars from last year provide the decor. Two pieces of wood, a rusted can and a rock are the children's toys. The time is now, the Gross National Product has just leaped another eight and a half percent, and the Steven Goodwater family has no shoes. Goodwater is an American Indian, and he is far worse off than his ancestors were when they went scalping the white man.

The Indian is still fighting. Seventy-six years after the Battle of Wounded Knee (his last military gasp), he is still trying to find his place in a land of people who remain as strange to him as when they walked west behind oxen. The Indian is at the absolute bottom of the totem pole. He dies at 43, 20 years before the rest of us. He lives on $30 a week (a black in Watts earns $64). He never got through grade school (half of all Indians drop out) and rarely has a job (40 to 75 percent, depending upon the locale, are unemployed) because there isn't any. His children are nearly twice as likely to die during infancy, and his entire family suffers from the infectious diseases that modern sanitation and health habits conquered a generation ago. He bitterly distrusts the government, yet clings childlike to its Bureau of Indian Affairs for help in virtually everything he does. He stands alone and confused, looking wistfully at his heritage, yet aware that the only way he is going to make it is in the white man's world. He is about as prepared to enter that world as he was at the turn of the century. Where is he going? Few seem to know.

The Indian Bureau, reshuffled still again last year, is regrouping, trying to draft a wide-ranging legislative proposal (it was due in January) that will satisfy knife-wielding critics and the half-million Indians in this country. One person who offers a sensible answer is half-Comanche and knows the Indian heartbreak. She is also the wife of Oklahoma's junior U.S. senator, and he provides the muscle behind her convictions. LaDonna Harris is tough, smart, angry. From that anger may grow a national realization that Indians should no longer be considered wards of the nation, but, instead, human beings with very human, basic problems.

END

PRODUCED BY CHARLES MANGEL

"SOMETIMES WE FEEL WE'RE ALREADY DEAD"

By Charles Mangel
LOOK Senior Editor

WE TALK, and the anguish goes on. We spend half a billion dollars each year on "the Indian problem" (enough to give each Indian family in the land a direct income of $6,000), yet three times as many Indian infants as white still die, more than twice as many children still quit school convinced they—not we—are dumb, ten times as many adults can't find work.

We don't even know where they all are. The 745 Cocopah Indians in Southwestern Arizona were not "discovered" by the Bureau of Indian Affairs until two years ago (although Selective Service had found them for World War II and conflicts since). The Cocopah may be the poorest tribe in the nation. Most still live in the ancestral mud-and-twig huts. Floors are dirt. Tree branches serve as fuel. Diseases the white man licked a generation ago are uncontrolled. The Cocopah continue to die young.

No road exists to link them to anything. You drive along the dirt bank of an irrigation canal. (During one rainstorm, an expectant mother had to get out of the ambulance bringing her to the hospital and help push the vehicle out of the mud.) The canal itself, conduit for the valuable water flowing to farmers inland, is neatly cemented and fenced, sharp contrast to the shanties lining its side. The desert grit cuts your eyes and seeps into your mouth and nose even after the car windows roll shut. The kids wipe uselessly at running noses with their sleeves. (Without adequate shelter, clothing, diet or medicine, Indian children remain the number-one victims of the respiratory infections that other Americans no longer consider dangerous.)

Jimmy Star lives in a hut 9 feet by 12 feet—about the size of a small rug—made of flattened cardboard cartons. The six-foot-high roof is cardboard, too, held down solely by two bald automobile tires. His income is $67 a month from welfare. The floor is the desert. He has no water, no toilet. A power line stands 50 feet from his paper door, but he doesn't have the $20 required to have it run to his home.

His neighbor, Bill Santez, is as desolate. Bill, 14, has just quit school. A quick boy with sensitive eyes, he could no longer accept the taunts of the white kids in Yuma, where he had attended public school. ("I don't drink. Why do they call me those names?") Abandoned by their parents, he and a brother a year younger, Bob, live with their grandmother. Bob has also quit school. ("Why stay there? I know a couple of Indians who went to college. They still can't get jobs.")

The nights are cold on the desert in the winter months, even in Arizona. Flames from a small fire in the center of the shack don't reach far. "We go to bed early," Bill says. "If you lay very still, it gets warm." Their house—mud and sticks on three sides and cardboard on the fourth—holds an old refrigerator. But it isn't used. "We just leave the food on the table," Bill explained. "It's cold enough."

Bill doesn't think he will go back to school. "They don't worry about us, just about the white ones. I asked a question one day. The teacher said, 'Stay in class and find out.' I told another teacher I was going to quit. He said, 'It's your own affair.'"

The two boys and their shrunken grandmother exist on an $85 monthly welfare check and the federal government's surplus-food program. Their diet is chiefly pinto beans, tortillas and potatoes. They rarely eat meat or fruit. I asked Bill about certain vegetables by name. He had not heard of half. "Don't you get tired of potatoes?" I asked. "Not as long as it fills my stomach." (Obesity is a major Indian problem, disguising malnutrition; the bulk of the Indian diet is starch.) A cough shook his body as he talked with me. He had had a cold for about four weeks. (With no exception, every one of the dozens of Cocopah children I found suffered from a respiratory illness; there is just no way it can be prevented.) Two calendars from 1963 decorate the walls. A Bible lay on a bed. "It's my brother's," Bill said. "He really believes in it."

The Indian belief in the Christian God is visible in the small Cocopah cemetery. Most of the graves are marked with simple wooden crosses. (Eight have carved head-markers. They are for veterans of our wars; the Veterans Administration paid for the stones.) The average age of the men lying there was 36. A Cocopah woman, chairman of the small tribal council, walked with me and told me about some of the men: Robert San Raphael, 36. "He died in a car accident." John Flower, 31. "He was my uncle. He was drinking too much. He died from that, I guess." (The average American Indian dies 20 years before the rest of us. The major cause of death: accidents—usually car accidents, believed related to drinking—followed by flu and pneumonia.) Woodrow Porrell, 26. "He drowned when he fell in the irrigation canal. He was drunk. He was my father." Henry Flower, John's brother, 39. "He shot himself. I think he was just tired of living." The oldest man in the cemetery was 54.

If anything, the Cocopah far exceed most of the "average" Indians in miseries. Their unemployment is an incredible nine out of ten men. Welfare keeps them alive, with a family income of about $1,000. Among the adolescents, virtually everyone I met had quit school. They desperately seek release from boredom and poverty. Indians have the highest suicide rate in the nation. Two young Cocopah killed themselves the month before I arrived. One was 16, the other, 18. Both had left school years before.

Timidity clouds the Cocopah future. Penniless, disorganized, they are uncertain of their own direction or of where to turn for aid. The BIA, under new and tougher local leadership, is beginning to stir, but slowly. (Ten houses—abandoned when a marine air base was closed—have been trucked in to one of the three different sites that comprise the Cocopah reservation.) The bedrock problems of schools and job training and employment remain untouched. Cocopah men and women, like Indians elsewhere, are slow to leave the reservations for jobs even if they have the skills and the perseverance to withstand employer prejudice (33 Indian men went to Yuma two years ago to enroll with the federal employment office; not one has yet been offered a job). The public schools to which most Indian children today are assigned clearly are failing them (eight Indians from one local school attempted junior college in the past few years; none could handle it).

The reticent, quiet Indian is getting angry. "The white man likes to meet and talk about our problems," says Henry Montague, Sr., tribal chairman of the neighboring Quechan, a larger tribe that tries to help the Cocopah as well as itself. "They call us once a year and listen and then send us home until next year."

Montague, a handsome, articulate man, stalked out of a recent meeting called by a platoon of government people. "We have a one-inch pipe that brings water into our reservation," Montague says. "At the end of the line, there just is no pressure. We have had to stand by helplessly while several houses there burned."

The Quechan had been pushing for ten months to get a larger line installed. "At this meeting," he said, "the talk went around and around. I finally got up and said, 'You are wasting my time. All you want to do is pass the buck.'" The Quechan have been battling federal authorities on the basics of land and water for more than a generation. The 95,000 acres granted them by government treaty in 1883 shrank to 50,000 the following year and to the present 9,000 nine years later. (Of 138 million acres held by American Indians in 1887, only 55 million remain in their hands today. The Sioux lost the Black Hills in South Dakota, for example, soon after prospectors discovered gold there.) The 1893 land grab from the Quechan was simply handled. The federal government decided the land should be held by individual tribe members, rather than the tribe as a whole. Leaders refused. They were jailed, beaten—and gave in. In the process of transfer from tribal to individual ownership (ten acres for each tribe member), 41,000 acres somehow became transferred to government control. The tribe has been trying since then to get 9,000 of those acres back.

Water, in the form of brimming irrigation canals, dissects the Quechan reservation. Yet the tribe cannot get more of it for itself. A carpet manufacturer, ready to employ 150 in a proposed plant on the reservation, had to be turned away because the Quechan could not promise the amount he needed. A private water supplier has a pipeline that has run through Quechan land for 40 years. He has no permission for a right-of-way and pays no fee. When the tribe's water pump broke down for two days last year, Montague had to get water from this man. The tribe paid $150.

Bill Santez passes the day playing mumblety-peg. He rarely lifts his eyes from his shoes. He will not go back to school, yet he has no plan of what he will do. He listens as a BIA man tells his grandmother that she will get a new house ("When?" she asks. "Maybe two years." "Oh, I die before then.") and then she tells me, "Sometimes we feel we're already dead."

The young principal of one of the schools the Indian children attend flops alongside me on a wooden chair. "These kids come to school at age five or six, and their eyes sparkle," he said." About the sixth grade, the dullness begins to creep in, and I know we've lost them."

We are losing most of our American Indians. And the question, unanswered since they and we put down our weapons, remains: What are we going to do about it? We still have not decided. We talk.

END

NINE "UNADOPTABLE" CHILDREN
JOINED BY LOVE

NINE OF THE ELEVEN CHILDREN in this family were born into emptiness. Each was abandoned at birth or soon after. And for each, a nightmarish existence followed. One lived alone on the streets of Korea for three years, until she was picked up at eight and taken to a settlement house. Another, a victim of 17 foster homes in her first five years of life, finally gave up and simply stopped talking to adults. A third child, of Ecuadorian-Indian parents, but taken for black, had acid thrown at her face during a southern racial incident. For three days, city officials hid her in hotel rooms while they feverishly tried to get her out of town. Finally, they shipped her north alone on a cargo plane. The pasts of the other six children match these. Each had another thing in common as well: No grown-ups wanted them. None but Julie and Kurt Lerke of Whitehouse, N.J., who found themselves unable to deny a child a chance at life.

The next time someone says kids are the same the world over, tell him about these nine children. Sarah hid in a field at five and watched Communist soldiers shoot her parents. For the next three years, she lived in the streets of Korea, sometimes with a gang of other homeless children, but usually alone. She was finally picked up by a U.S. Army nurse and started on the journey that brought her to New Jersey. It was two years before her nightmares stopped, and she could have an uninterrupted night's sleep.

John was adopted from a Korean orphanage when he was 10 months old. He weighed 10 pounds, about right for a six-week-old infant. He screamed day and night for the first month. Mrs. Lerke spent most of her days holding him in her arms. He pressed himself to her so violently that, by evening, her face had the imprint of his.

Charles was so pitifully weak an Army doctor advised that he be left in Korea to die. He was flown across the Pacific in a box intended to be his coffin if he did not survive the trip.

After five years in 17 different foster homes in three states, Mary Jane was placed in two homes for adoption and rejected both times. Once extremely affectionate, she had already stopped talking to adults. Her eyes never left the ground. (She expressed herself in other ways. During her first hour with the Lerkes, she shoved Charlie off the top of a bunk bed, shearing off two of his teeth.)

Amanda had been settled in a white foster home in a Southern city. White racists, interpreting the presence of this dark-skinned Ecuadorian-Indian, seven years old, as an attempt to integrate the neighborhood, forced her out of three different foster homes in three days. The acid was thrown during their last successful eviction. It missed by inches. When Amanda reached Whitehouse three days later, Mrs. Lerke found "fear still running out of her eyes."

Son of a Korean mother unable to care for him and, probably, of a black father, Michael had been virtually on his own in this country since he was five. En route to Newark (N.J.) Airport to meet the Lerkes, he told the social worker accompanying him, "No one will be there."

Edith was in the care of welfare officials in the same Southern city where Amanda lived. When the Lerkes asked to adopt her, they were turned down. A white child, they were told, could not be sent to a home housing mixed-race children. Edith went to an all-white family in the north. When this family was unable to cope with her truculence after three weeks, they asked that she be removed. Welcome House, the adoption agency that had taken responsibility for Edith, called and told the Lerkes about her. Born to a Korean mother and father, Margaret was adopted with Charlie. She was seven months old and weighed five pounds.

Susan was so tanned from exposure that she was thought to be black. Her mother was Korean and her father, white. Her scalp was covered with mange and lice.

The children came to the Lerkes within a relatively short span of time: two in 1957, two in 1958 and five in a rush during a 20-month period ending in September 1963. Adjustment was torturous. For a long time, all Julie and Kurt Lerke and their natural children—Katherine, now 19, married and living nearby, and Todd, 14—could do was be patient. (Mike spent the first three months slamming doors.) The previously adopted children, with their special understanding of each newcomer's torments, helped. Edith, shaken after her dismissal by prospective parents, and moody in her fears that it would happen again, found John, seven, waiting for her one morning as she left for school. "Don't worry," he told her. "Anyone who comes to this house never has to leave."

The Lerkes could have become foster parents and accepted child-support checks. Receiving would have been the easier way. Instead, they chose adoption and paid fees and expenses averaging $800 to get each child. The year the first child came, Lerke, a stock-room supervisor in an electronics plant, began to supplement his income with part-time work. A large vegetable garden was started behind the eight-room house and laying hens were purchased to reduce food bills.

To a recent guest who expressed awe at the adoption of nine children, considered by many to be unadoptable, Mrs. Lerke, a former teacher, replied matter-of-factly, "We are doing nothing we don't want to do. This is a family, not a project." A family it is. The nightmares and dark moods have been replaced by a serenity rarely seen in children. Each of the adopted Lerkes has seemingly developed a calm tolerance for the trivia that beset most youngsters. They are children and still cry, but not over a snapped kite string or a misappropriated baseball. Each has been accepted into the community without reservation. The entire family, with the exception of four-year-old Suzy, joins vigorously in every activity Whitehouse offers, from choir in the century-old Methodist Church to the PTA.

As this story was being written, the Lerkes were called by an adoption agency about an 11-month-old mulatto girl. No home could be found for her, and an orphanage seemed the only answer. Would the Lerkes adopt a tenth child? Kurt Lerke asked the agency to keep trying, but added, "If you can't find anyone, please call us back." When he hung up, he turned to his wife, "How can we tell a child we have no more room here?"

END

PRODUCED BY CHARLES MANGEL

MY LONGEST DAY

A war correspondent on June 6, 1944, in Normandy, Cornelius Ryan realized how little anyone knew of what was occurring, and decided that day to write about it. The Longest Day became a monumental best-selling book, and, later, a film. Now, ten years after his book, the author is trapped. He has become confessor, counselor, lost and found department, post office and repository of memories for D-Day veterans. Here, Ryan, in a taped interview with Look senior editor Charles Mangel, talks about his 25-year involvement in one of the decisive days of history.

ON THE GREAT INVASION FLEET, some soldiers slept like babies, as though the dawn would be like any other. I remember, some wrote letters, some played cards, some rolled dice and, here and there, men prayed. Some huddled in little groups, trying to make conversation, but most had long since run out of anything new to say. Some gazed into the darkness, waiting for the dawn and that first glimpse of Normandy.

The hours dragged on. Suddenly, the transports stopped. There was the rattle of anchor chains. But it was still dark. Was Normandy out there somewhere in front? Slowly, very slowly, darkness gave way to dawn. Now men strained to see what lay ahead. In the haze, the coastline took shape, a low silhouette shrouded in gray mist, pierced in places by the blackness of a cliff or low ground rising gently to become a roll of green hills. And that innocent-looking strip where the sea ended and the land began snaked across the coastline like a piece of cotton. That was the unknown and the finality. That was the beach.

We have this idea about D-Day: Out of the dawn, a million men plowed ashore through the surf, flags flying, and marched on to Berlin.

Ridiculous. Less than 9,000 men landed on a 50-mile stretch in the first wave. They came in a thin, straggly line of landing craft, odd-looking matchboxes bobbing about in a very rough sea, a gray sort of morning, terribly misty. Above them, those enormous white puffs rolled out from the guns of the battleships, following their shells.

Yet the invasion was strictly Madison Avenue. The organization was fantastic. Five thousand ships; fifteen thousand planes; hundreds of correspondents. You couldn't help asking yourself: What's the other fellow thinking about? What's he doing? Has anyone considered the villagers along the coast? What were the Allied soldiers thinking? How many Germans did they see? What did the Free French feel as they fired at their homeland? What were the Germans doing? Were they as ill as our men? Did they pray too? Did they eat too?

I felt a total inadequacy trying to report. I felt angry that there was no way to tell the story without getting inside the men who were living it. In some vague, unformed way, I knew I had to get this down on paper. I had to be able to say, "This is the way it was." If I'd been a soldier, I might have had a kind of cynicism. I might not have been interested in finding out why. But I was just young enough, just eager enough to be mad at myself for not really knowing. I determined to find out the stupid things, the mad things, the courageous things. I simply had to know—that was all.

But D-Day ended and I joined Patton's Third Army. After Europe, I was ordered to the Far East. The book did not come back to me until 1949, when a group of the original correspondents returned to Normandy for D-Day's fifth anniversary. I walked along the beach and began to look at the garbage of war still there: burned-out vehicles, weapons. I remember watching a fisherman drag a howitzer out of the sea with his net. A skeleton, helmet on correctly, was tangled up somehow with the cannon's wheels. Who was he? Nobody, nobody anywhere, knew which men had landed on D-Day in the first wave. What an appalling thing. I understood it; who had the time to record such incidentals? Seriously now, I began to think about writing the book.

By then, I was working for *Collier's*. I couldn't get them, or anyone else, interested. So I started on my own time, spending my own money.

I began searching for records, people. I ran advertisements: "Where were you on June 6, 1944? Contact me if you took part in D-Day." I began writing to survivors. Eventually, I sent out 6,000 questionnaires. Two thousand came back. Out of these came 700 interviews, about half by me. Some 240 books had already appeared on D-Day. I read them all. I began to fill large notebooks with contradictions. There were many.

This was the pattern through December 1956. *Collier's* went out of business. I was already about $20,000 in debt for travel, correspondence, translations. My wife Kathryn was then an editor with *House and Home*. We decided that I should devote full-time to the book. I began writing. I took the first pages to Simon & Schuster and got a small advance from them. Still, at the time, no magazine would buy serial rights, and thus provide money.

About the middle of 1957, I realized I didn't have nearly enough research. That discovery terrified me. I had enough research if I was prepared to take the stuff baldly, without verifying reports. But I didn't have enough research to write as accurately as history demanded. I had discovered so much that was new. If I didn't nail things down, I would be laughed out of business by the academic fraternity. For example: Rommel wasn't at his post when the invasion began. He had gone back to Germany for his wife's birthday. The Allied codes for D-Day had been broken by the Germans. Back of the beach dunes, the Canadians had slit their prisoners' throats in retaliation for Dieppe. I had to make sure all this was true. So I decided I would use no story unless the facts were corroborated by at least two other eyewitnesses or recorded in some kind of official report.

I had to be sure about the mysteries I was turning up. Why were all the German beachhead commanders called from their stations the day before the invasion for war games far inland? Why were all but *two* fighter planes pulled out of Normandy the week before? Why did no German—with reconnaissance, radar or in submarines—see that vast invasion fleet building up in British ports or crossing the Channel? Who were those shadowy men seen on the beaches the night before the invasion? Why did the Germans, after getting a patrol down to the water between the American and British beachheads, withdraw rather than send a force there in sufficient strength to roll up the Allies' flank? Why were there no births or deaths among the French in Normandy on June 6? And who, when the first American Ranger scratched his way to the top of a nine-story cliff searching for gun emplacements, had written there for him to see: "Kilroy was here"? This additional checking now began to double the research, the expense and the time. (It also cost a lot of superb material that I believed but was unable to verify.)

I finished in August 1959. I had no idea what would happen. Kathryn and I had worked seven days a week with absolutely no time off for at least the previous three or four years. Even though I finally received financial and research help from the *Reader's Digest*, we were still about $60,000 in debt. I turned the manuscript in and walked immediately over to the *Digest* to ask for an assignment. Then I went home, and Kathryn and I stared at each other. All of a sudden, we didn't know what to do with ourselves.   Not for long.

Late one night, shortly after the book came out, there was a knock on our apartment door in New York. A man stood in the hall. "Your name is Ryan?" he asked. "Yes." "Can I talk to you?" "Well, sure. What's it about?" "I was with the 82nd Airborne. I have to talk to you." The man came in. "I've had this on my mind for 15 years. I must tell somebody." Soon after D-Day, this man, a private, had been walking down a side road in Normandy with his sergeant and his corporal. Suddenly, there was a burst of–perhaps–mortar fire. The corporal fell with half his head blown off, but he was still talking. The private and the sergeant stopped and looked at him. The private said to the sergeant, "We can't leave him like this." The man was still mumbling, his limbs still jerking. The sergeant said, "He's all yours. I'm going up the road." My visitor turned to me and whispered, "I killed that man, Mr. Ryan."

These were perhaps the worst of what was to come–the confessions. So much guilt. So much remorse. A young Midwestern enlisted man in the 101st Airborne went through the entire invasion and all through France without firing a shot. He didn't see a German until he got to the Elbe River. The first Germans he saw weren't Germans. They were

Americans returning from a patrol, and he machined-gunned nine of them dead. This man today is a wreck, an alcoholic. He can't hold a job. He writes at least four or five times a year. He visits me. He rang the bell one day with his latest wife. She was drunker than he. Poor Kathryn had to put them up for the weekend.

Our soldiers, like all soldiers, were trained to a razor edge: "Do your job; that's the only objective." Responding, men became killers. One American paratrooper I spoke with prowled from area to area, out of his own unit's vicinity, like a will-o'-the-wisp during and after the invasion. He didn't shoot Germans. He just sneaked up behind them and slit their throats. He was "doing his job." I get a letter about every three months from him. He tells me what he's doing, brings me up to date and always winds up by saying, "Of course, I wasn't able to hold that job for too long, you understand." He had been overtrained, came out a killer and has not been able to readjust. I have had at least 20 or 30 of these men come to me since the book was published with similar stories.

Of course, confessions were part of the book research too. As word got around that I was working on *The Longest Day*, I would begin to get letters, something like this: "Dear Mr. Ryan. My husband [or father] is a shy man and I know he would never tell his story to you. But you've got to talk with him. He landed with the first wave." Days later, I would receive a strangulated telephone call: "Ah, Mr. Ryan, this is very embarrassing. I understand my wife [or daughter] wrote to you. Look, I don't know how to put this, but I didn't land on D-Day. I've been talking about it, but...." So I now admit for the first time that there are nine ringers listed in the "D-Day Veterans" section at the back of the book. Their accounts are not in the story, but their names are in this index. What was I to do? I just had to leave the names in. (Years later, when I told General Eisenhower what I had done and why, he said, "If you hadn't done it, I wouldn't have let you interview me again.")

A German major broke down and cried in front of me and two interpreters while I was interviewing him. He was Pluskat, the man in the beach bunker who had looked out at dawn and saw that incredible invasion fleet. He called his headquarters and tried to report. "You're crazy, Pluskat," he was told. "The Allies don't have that many ships *in the world.*" Pluskat lost his temper. The man at headquarters finally said, "Well, which way are those ships heading, Pluskat?" And Pluskat, speaking for the whole German army, said, "Right for *me.*" When I talked with Pluskat, he broke down. He firmly believed that he had failed as a soldier because he had not been able to convince his headquarters that D-Day had begun.

The flow of visitors finally convinced us to give up our New York apartment. Now, long afterward, we still get 50 or 60 people coming to our suburban home every year, enlisted men and generals. A repairman fixing the refrigerator turns out to be a veteran of the Ninth Army. We chew the fat. The upholsterer who called for a sofa had been at the Elbe. I listen to his story.

Many of the men are so bitter, so angry still, a quarter of a century later. They were important for one fleeting day. I have argued for years for a special citation to be issued to the men of the first three waves. Theirs was a very special battle, with a very special purpose that put them a little apart from those who stormed Africa, Sicily, Tarawa. Their target was Hitler's Fortress Europe, and these men from all the Allied countries *just could not fail.* Today, middle-aged, they feel frustrated, forgotten. It's sad.

Perhaps the first real glimpse I had of response to the book was the mail that began to pour in immediately after publication. I received letters from kids, something like this: "I'm a high school student. I read about my father in your book. I knew he had landed on D-Day, but he doesn't talk about it much. For the first time I learned what it was all about, about my father, and what it means to be an American. Bless you." Or the letter from the woman who had married a simple, quiet guy. After a while, she thought him just a colorless, dull man. She read in the book that he had been a hero among heroes, and she wrote to say that suddenly she saw him in a different light.

I would get letters from divorced people: "If I had known this about my husband, I would never have left him. Can you put me in touch with him?" Of course, I got the reverse too: "You mentioned Sergeant John Doe. Where is the old son of a bitch? I married him in 1942 and haven't seen him since."

One young woman wrote that her father had been killed on D-Day. She said, "All my life, I hated my father because I didn't have him. It wasn't until I read *The Longest Day* that I realized what my father had given to his country, to me. All of a sudden, I *did* have a father." A mother wanted to tell us what had happened to her son, a Ranger who had been among the first to land. After D-Day, he was paralyzed in action and died, ten years later, at 32, as a result of the wound. "The nurses said he prayed constantly ... and they thought that was such a nice way to go since so many of the boys [in the veterans hospital] were so embittered they went out swearing."

The mail fit virtually every category. An American physician wrote. He had been trying desperately since war's end to find his kid brother, a German pilot. A woman in Romania asked if a German officer in the book could possibly be her missing brother. He was, and we helped them meet. (We have helped to bring a number of families together.) American women requested the addresses of Germans in the book who fascinated them. Three thousand letters poured in the first year from perhaps 15 countries. Many were addressed just to "Cornelius Ryan, *The Longest Day*." They are still coming, perhaps 1,000 a year. Last week alone, I counted 74 letters from high school and college students asking for help on school papers. We answer every letter the best way we can.

I have wondered why the attention continues in such intensity, why the book sold so well everywhere. Perhaps it has something to do with the rash of books—novels—that began to be issued after the end of the war: sadism, sex, psychoanalytic messages. *The Longest Day* told about people caught up in conflict; men I call knights who did their best, and this was called courage. William Faulkner, in his Nobel Prize acceptance speech, said it is the "writer's ... privilege to help man endure by lifting his heart, by reminding him of the courage and honor and hope and pride and compassion and pity and sacrifice which have been the glory of his past." I've tried to show that man can and will prevail even under the worst circumstances. That was the story of D-Day: of individuals who did what had to be done to save our world. I tried to report it. Their success was the book's success. That's why I dedicated it to "the men of D-Day."

Does this sound odd so many years later? Behind Omaha Beach there's a cemetery with 9,000 GI's in it. On one of the crosses is a parent's inscription: "Into the great mosaic of victory, this priceless jewel was set." I have tried to write about jewels.

END

PAUL DOUGLAS: MAN AHEAD OF HIS TIME

By Charles Mangel
LOOK Senior Editor

His face could have been an Indian chieftain's. The nose is grandly hooked. The forehead and cheekbones are high and prominent. His hair, now gray-white, is a high and narrow thatch. His socks droop, occasionally below the anklebone. His shoes, rarely on, are scuffed. His shirttail is never in. His hats have no front or back. Shapeless and crushed, each sits atop his head much as an untidy bird's nest adorns a mountain crag. He is tall, and heavy, and when he stands, he lurches slightly off-center, more a lean to his right than a stoop.

He is as implausible in character as in appearance. Although few would go with him, he rose on the floor of the United States Senate to announce his finances because "people have a right to know where my money comes from." Left arm made useless by World War II machine-gun and mortar wounds, he refuses a large disability pension because, he says, he is able to work. He took up causes when the country was ducking them (were you doing anything about civil rights in 1949 or Medicare in 1950?) and fought many through to eventual victory. He challenged pork-barrel legislation in his home state and campaigned for open housing in areas where people were winging rocks at Negroes. He drafted the Senate's first penalty-laden Code of Ethics, has demanded its adoption since he helped investigate the Reconstruction Finance Corporation scandal in 1950-1951. He says Congress will someday be forced to adopt a code.

Paul H. Douglas of Illinois, beaten for reelection last fall by age, the white backlash and Republican Charles H. Percy, may be judged in time one of the most gifted men in the history of the Senate.

In his 18 Washington years, Douglas demonstrated an ability to find and voice national issues before other men were aware of them--or ready for them. He introduced civil-rights legislation in 1949, his first year in Washington, was one of the leaders in the campaign for passage of the 1957 Civil Rights Act, the first approved in 82 years, and introduced strengthening proposals every session afterward. His ideas during this period became the quarry from which the comprehensive 1964 act and the 1965 changes were mined. Clarence Mitchell, NAACP boss in Washington, told me bluntly: "Without Paul Douglas, we would have no civil-rights legislation as we know it today. He was the leader of the Senate team from 1949 into the early '60's."

Douglas first proposed federally supported health insurance for catastrophic illness in 1950 and followed with a broader Medicare proposal in 1960. The National Council of Senior Citizens, following Medicare's passage in 1965, recognized him and Clinton Anderson as the two senators who did most to make the program possible.

Douglas was an author of the amendment to the Social Security Act that established disability insurance for men younger than 65. (In 1935, he had been summoned from the University of Chicago to help write the nation's original Social Security law.)

He was the Senate floor manager for the first Federal slum-clearance and urban-renewal program, which became law in 1949. He later became a principal sponsor of most of the important housing legislation of the last decade.

He originated the "pockets of poverty" thesis in the Senate, sponsored the area-redevelopment program, first national effort at aiding depressed communities, and its successor, the 1965 Economic Development Act.

Following a Senate inquiry into fraud in union and company pension-fund management that led two men to prison, Douglas drafted the first Federal legislation, in 1958, requiring disclosure of the handling of the billions in these funds.

In 1959, Douglas and the Joint Economic Committee that he chaired began a nine-month examination of the national economy-growth, employment and price stabilization. (The economy at that point was stagnant. During the 1953-60 period, the U.S. had suffered three recessions, the rate of real economic growth was running below that of virtually every major country in the world, and unemployment was rising--it reached seven percent of the work force by early 1961, highest since the Depression. Overall prices were climbing at an average 2.6 percent annually.) This kind of detailed analysis by a team of trained economists had never been undertaken before. Recommendations stemming from the study played a major role in the adoption of policies that, before escalation began in Vietnam, fostered the longest and strongest peacetime expansion in the country's history.

A voting independent who sought issues, not party positions, Douglas was willing to take on the "impossible" battles years away from winning (something you don't do when you want to pile up a legislative record) and not worry about the disinclination of his peers to join him. Yet Vice-President Humphrey could later say, "...No member of the Senate...has his name stamped on more major issues... and major legislation than Paul Douglas."

Intellectual, self-effacing, highly emotional (at times, perhaps uncontrollably so), Douglas was both teacher and catalyst. He saw no reason why he should not rise frequently, alone if need be, to tell the Senate what he thought it should do. This was scarcely a posture to gain popularity, either in the Democratic Party or the Senate. But it was very much in keeping with the man, who came to Washington, at 56, with a national reputation as an economist and as a war hero.

The current honesty mess splattering both houses of Congress is a case in point. Slack standards permitted the misconduct of Baker, Dodd and Powell. The situation could be drastically different if our representatives had the deep-down guts to enact two basic reforms.

Douglas sketched the simple solutions when I visited him in Washington and New York: 1) tax-paid national election campaigns; 2) annual, audited disclosure by members of Congress (and high appointed officials) of their capital holdings, their income and its sources.

"The hesitation of congressional leaders to carry out any strong cleanup policy naturally leads the public to believe that the revealed sins of the few are the predominant practices of the many," he said. (A recent

Gallup poll reported that six of ten Americans asked believe misuse of funds by congressmen is "fairly common.")

Douglas, tired at 75, but with spirit still blazing, wasted no time in pinpointing for me the central problem-campaign funds. "These costs are no longer under control. It was estimated that Mr. [Nelson] Rockefeller's last campaign cost $5,000,000. That's an extraordinary amount of money for an ordinary man to raise. A candidate must be wealthy or look for wealthy benefactors. Few large benefactors give without expectation of a later harvest."

The harvest comes in many forms: special laws that punch loopholes in the tax structure, government contracts, subsidies, quotas for special industry groups. "The public is paying for the elections *right now* by having to absorb these extra costs," Douglas says. Plugging of tax loopholes alone, he would argue in the perennial fight he led for tax reform, *would allow the tax rate to be cut in half, yet raise the same amount of revenue.* ("Last year," he said in one floor debate, "a charwoman earning $55 a week paid more in income taxes than an oil company whose income was $26 million.")

Douglas knows that legislators live the year round "in a very real world where very real economic pressures operate." Expensive campaigns "place tremendous strain on a man who does not have much money." Political expenses continue between elections: trips home, beyond the allowance for that item; maintenance, sometimes, of two homes; purchase of tapes for radio and TV reports; political contributions; entertainment of constituents. These expenses cost Douglas $12,382 in 1966. And out of a congressional salary of $30,000, he ended up with a net of less than $7,000 to cover all living costs.

(Douglas, who began to disclose his annual income and its sources when he first held political office as a reform Chicago alderman in 1939, says that if he had not been able to earn extra income-- $8,285 last year from lectures, book royalties and articles--he could not have remained in the Senate.)

All this time, influence money is available. "Congressmen have more opportunities for temptation thrown their way in a year than the average person does in a lifetime," Douglas told me. Shortly after he was elected in 1948, he began to receive valuable gifts, many from strangers. He sent them back and established a policy of accepting nothing worth more than $2.50. "It's a silly place to draw the line but it must be put somewhere, and I don't think a senator can be bought for less than $2.50."

"It would be far cheaper, "Douglas wrote in his book, *Ethics in Government,* "if the government met the costs of the campaigns, since then the elected officials and parties would not be under obligation to the big contributors. [They] would be able to act and to legislate far more freely in the public interest.... The vast majority of politicians, like most men, desire in their hearts to be good public servants and they fall short of this ideal, largely to the degree to which they have been trapped by the terrific pressures of political life."

Annual disclosure by members of Congress and appointed officials above a certain salary, he believes, is essential both for public assurance and as a "disinfectant."

"Publicity is a powerful deterrent from improper conduct. Most men [who go wrong do so] because they think they can commit shady acts in private, which will not be found out."

Douglas is convinced the level of honesty in both houses of Congress is good, "a good deal higher than the general level in our society," and steadily rising. "There is much less chicanery than people think."

He finds it difficult to condemn his former colleagues. "I would try to have the public realize its lack of appreciation of the difficulties politicians face. While I think I have kept myself clean--God knows I've tried--I am struck with the enormous continuing pressures to which politicians are subjected--pressures far greater than those which people in private life are subjected to. A meaningful honesty code and bill will have to be passed sooner or later. Congress increasingly will see that it is the only way out of the financial pressures growing around it-- and the public will demand it."

Reforms, Douglas knows well, come slowly. In a 1964 report to his constituents, he drew two major points: "1) long periods of public education are needed before these issues are accepted; 2) I see my own role...primarily as one of introducing and trying to develop these much needed but controversial issues so that they eventually gain success."

One example illustrates. Douglas came to the Senate knowing how much the nation had to do in civil rights and tore into the issue in his maiden speech two months after. He tried repeatedly but failed to get an effective measure on to the floor. In 1956, after seven years, the House at last passed a bill and Douglas pleaded with the Senate to take it up. It was July, and hot, and the senators wanted to get on to the national conventions. Douglas insisted, and finally, in a vote on whether or not to allow the bill to be discussed, he was humiliated, 76-6. It was the "worst moment" of a Senate career. He turned and walked out of the chamber. At the door, he met Muriel Humphrey. Her husband, a good friend and supporter of many Douglas causes, had voted against him. Douglas bent and kissed Mrs. Humphrey. Then he continued to his office and wept for two hours. Yet the next year, a bill was passed, and better ones followed.

The causes Douglas undertook he fought for with a depth of commitment that all but his severest foes admitted and respected. (one of his bitterest opponents, the late Sen. Robert S. Kerr, turned to him in exasperation after a Douglas-Kerr floor fight and asked, in effect, whether Douglas considered himself to be Jesus Christ.) Sitting in his drab New York City hotel room, I asked Douglas what had guided him in the Senate. He wiggled his toes (the shoes were off again) and answered without hesitation: "I wanted to represent the general public interest. It is frequently not represented. The power establishment in the Senate is on the whole biased against the public interest. The small taxpayers--people of low income, of minority groups--are individually weak. The special interests, producing interests, are...organized. In the struggle between concentrated private interest and diffused general interest, the private interests have all the resources and drive they need to win."

This clearly underscored Douglas's concern. His nonstop battle to cut budget waste was an attempt not only to save money but to get some of it used for what he called "human needs," such as more aid to education.

In budget paring, he far outdid his conservative colleagues. (A liberal, he declared, "does not have to be a wastrel.")

Douglas failed, by self-admission, in one area and succeeded spectacularly in another. The first, pork barrel, utterly threw him. "I just had to give up. I couldn't take it any longer. For about ten years, I hit my head against a...wall. The people want it; they expect it; heaven help the legislator who does not deliver."

But for two-thirds of his Washington years, Douglas lectured the pork barrelers, including his own constituents and senators who called for cuts in spending everywhere but home. "As groups win their battle for special expenditures," he said in one of the 13 books he has written, "they lose the more important war for general economy...They are like drunkards who shout for temperance in the intervals between cocktails."

Somewhat of a ham, Douglas once took a magnifying glass and atlas on to the Senate floor to try to find some of the geographic hideaways designated for pork-barrel cash. Or he would stand, as he did one year, and calmly announce, "There is a provision for $50,400 to aid small boars and construct a landing for a ferry in Illinois. But, gentlemen, the ferry stopped running in 1945."

Another time, with the budget $5 billion in the red, Douglas charged that of the $1.8 billion proposed for rivers, harbors and flood-control projects, $830 million was waste.

Item: $918,000 to dredge, and $18,000 a year to maintain, a Georgia-Florida river. Beneficiaries: A paper mill that would save $135,000 in annual freight charges; a second mill that would save $14,000.

A senator once rose to petition for aid to crabs. Several inlets in his state, he submitted, should be dredged so "the motorboats wouldn't roil the crabs." A weary Douglas piped up: "Must we extend welfare-state benefits to crustacean life?"

The successes came after hopeless years of whacking at defense profligacy. "The military authorities," he held, "are probably the greatest wasters of manpower and materials in the country." He charged, ten years in a row, that a minimum of $2 billion to $3 billion annually could be saved by the armed services through unification of supply systems, a jump in competitively bid contracts from an appallingly low 11.9 percent, and on and on. He was ignored.

Douglas's 1960 assault caused an uproar. Arms loaded, he marched into the Senate one June afternoon and held up a lamp socket the Navy had purchased for $21.10. He had bought the identical socket in a store for 25 cents. The Air Force had purchased an operator's headset for $10.67. Douglas had had the same item made in a neighborhood electronics store for $1.50. The list ran through eight more items. As proof, Douglas had copies of the actual invoices used.

The Defense Department denied everything. One item, it claimed, had been bought as an "experimental or specialized design." Douglas dug into his briefcase and flourished a copy of the patent for the device, dated 12 years earlier. Douglas "urge[d] the Congress and the Budget Bureau and the President…to knock some heads together." The heads went unknocked.

The situation reversed when Robert S. McNamara moved into the Pentagon. McNamara picked up suggestions made by a Douglas subcommittee and blended them with his own streamlining efforts. Savings in the Defense Department in fiscal 1965: $4.8 *billion*. Said McNamara, in making that announcement: "The Department of Defense cost-reduction program… owes much of its inspiration to… Senator Douglas…."

It may take generations to total the billions saved for the United States by the actions of Douglas, acting alone or as group leader. His fight against the grab of a national resource, offshore oil, by the states may yield the biggest payoff. In 1953, four states attempted to get ownership of *all* offshore oil and gas rights (they already had part of these rights). Congress was asked to overturn Supreme Court decisions giving ownership to the Federal government. Douglas, in alliance with Lister Hill of Alabama, held off the states' righters on the Senate floor for 30 days. He presented a detailed 52-page argument, jammed with charts, to illustrate "a give-away beyond belief."

"Most of the sponsors of this bill," he said, "are the very ones who say they are gravely concerned about the size and burden of the public debt, yet this bill would alienate assets which may ultimately be equal in value to that debt and could be used to reduce it. We are concerned with the 2 ½ million illiterates in this country and the low level of education given to others, yet this bill would throw away a large future income which could be used to wipe out illiteracy and help ensure to all an acceptable minimum of education."

After 30 days, the bill's sponsors abruptly threw in the sponge. A compromise gave the states title only up to three miles out (Texas picked up seven more miles). Because they thought all the underwater oil was close to shore, the bill's backers advertised the compromise, which passed, as a victory. They were wrong. Most of the oil located so far lies beyond the state limits. The Federal treasury has already taken in $1 billion in royalties. Experts think the total may hit $40 billion. In addition, the nation has title to the increasingly valuable gas and mineral rights for the same areas.

Some of Douglas's battles will have to be won by others. Among them: His nine-year fight, strongly opposed by lending interests, for a truth-in-lending bill that would require those who routinely offer credit to reveal the real annual interest rate and the total cost of interest and fees.

Yet he is not keeping himself out of the legislative world. He was the leadoff witness twice at recent Senate hearings, besides maintaining a pace that perhaps has intensified since he left the Old Senate Office Building. He divides his time between the chairmanship of the National Commission on Urban Problems, teaching and lecturing at the New School for Social Research in New York City and anchoring a television interview program.

Douglas traveled a solitary path in the Senate, and it was inevitable. "Beneath the surface of a senator's life is a deep loneliness," he says, "[because] when the chips are down…, a man should vote his profound individual convictions…regardless of who is with him or against him. I never tried to make a fetish of being independent for its own sake. But if you do what you think is right, no one, no criticism can injure you." One of Douglas's oldest Senate enemies laughs at this. He told me, "I never saw an issue that could not stand compromise." Douglas might smile at the comment and recall lost battles that turned into wars won because he anchored a belief long enough for others to join him.

"In every generation," a New York *Times* editorial said of Douglas, "there are a few men who by force of mind and character become moral exemplars to their contemporaries, the standard by which other men in public life measure their conduct." Every man is more than the sum of his visible work. The quality of Douglas cannot be measured by the legislation he conceived or helped push through or the money he helped to save or redirect to better purpose. He was always a curious blend: a Phi Beta Kappa who played varsity football at Bowdoin, a rigidly moral man who turned down the chairmanship of the Dodd investigating committee ("I'm not virtuous enough to judge any man"), an economist who could stand before a hippy group of college students and say: "...what is needed most in the world is love.... Truth has at once a compulsive and healing power; we should not be afraid of truth for...it is the rock upon which we can base our....lives.... Human courage in defense of an ideal is an ultimate virtue...."

Some years back, Douglas wrote this about character: "It is not hard in solitude to wish all mankind well, but the test is whether we do in fact visit the sick, feed the hungry, clothe the naked and protect the weak.... There are many who profess their devotion to the common good, but the test is whether they are willing...to ring the doorbells of an indifferent citizenry and to brave the opposition...of entrenched greed."

The Senate will miss Douglas.

END

Book Excerpts

From "Something's Wrong with My Child"

Three Children

These are the true stories of three learning-disabled youngsters. They illustrate the great variety of ways this handicap can affect children.

Unable to work at his classmates' first-grade level, Timmy allows no one else to work. Four doctors, one a psychiatrist, have said he is emotionally disturbed, but a year of expensive therapy has not helped. Guilt-ridden and desperate to the point of sleeplessness, his parents are leaning to the advice of one of the physicians, who has said, "There's nothing more you can do. Put him in a home."

The day after that counsel, the mother, Theresa Anderson, waited until her husband had left for work, took his pistol from the bedroom closet shelf, loaded it, and called her three young children into the living room. She lined them up in front of the fireplace–Jon, eight, Timmy, six, Susan, three–and prepared to kill each of them and then herself.

Mrs. Anderson, intelligent, well educated, and to all appearances a good mother, could take no more of Timmy. "It got to the point where I began to doubt my own sanity."

The boy's supercharged behavior was destroying his family. His parents were on the verge of separation. His school, in a large suburb of New York City, was threatening to have him committed–at the age of six–to a reformatory, for "incorrigibility." He roamed around his classroom, disturbing children near him, ignoring his teacher's requests. He shrieked when irritated, regardless of time or place. He bit and hit without provocation. Mrs. Anderson had been called repeatedly to the principal's office. During one visit, the principal said, "I hope you realize how much of a problem your family has been to us. We just don't have time for a child like yours." "The impression was clear," said Mrs. Anderson later. "I was too ignorant to raise a child; if I used some discipline on my son, he might behave."

The children waited obediently. Mrs. Anderson, pistol held behind her back, stood in front of them. She finally turned and ran upstairs, the children still in an orderly row before the living-room fireplace.

The following week, the Andersons placed Timmy in a state-run home for the emotionally disturbed. He was to remain there for four years.

Timmy had kicked out the slats of his crib at eleven months and had been in constant motion ever since. "Every night I had to make fifteen or twenty trips upstairs to get him back into his crib," says Mrs. Anderson. "Finally, in frustration, I tied him spread-eagled to his crib with my husband's belts. I sat downstairs and cried, and he cried upstairs. Just to get dinner on the table for the other children, I had to tie him to the living-room railing each night with rope."

Housework was done around midnight, when Timmy would doze for a couple of hours. He never slept through the night. Mrs. Anderson "crept around" quietly washing the floors, doing laundry and her other chores, fearful the noise would wake Timmy.

Mr. Anderson simply fled from the problem. To escape his home, he worked almost constantly. He and his wife never went out. Timmy's parents refused all invitations to other people's homes. ("If I didn't go, I would not have to return the invitation.") Their daughter "developed a deep hatred for Timmy and for me," Mrs. Anderson said. "She deliberately belittled him."

At the age of two, Timmy hurled toys at his mother whenever anything frustrated him. He could not be left alone. "One day he went out to ride his bike," his mother said. "I found out by hearing car after car screech to a halt to avoid this little kid riding his tricycle in the busy street in front of our home. He just seemed to have no common sense. He never seemed to look ahead, to realize the consequences of his actions."

He once took a garden hose lying in front of a neighbor's home, turned it on, and sprayed water through the front door of the neighbor's house. A little girl who lived nearby came out one day, wearing a party dress, to wait for her parents. Timmy jumped with both feet into a mud puddle right next to the girl. His sister had a newly born kitten. His mother once caught him playing with the kitten by throwing it up in the air and letting it fall on the concrete basement floor. Timmy didn't seem to realize that he was hurting the kitten.

"I don't understand how this boy is alive today," his mother said. "We put him to bed one night at eight, and he kept getting up and wandering around bothering his sister. Finally, at eleven, my husband had reached the end of his patience. He raced up to Timmy in his sister's room, grabbed him by the neck of his pajamas, and threw him into his bed. He almost strangled him accidentally. He did do some damage to the neck cartilage."

Timmy had no fear. The day of a televised moon launch, his mother found him playing astronaut. He was about to jump out of a second-floor window. His parents put bars on his windows and a lock and chain on his bedroom door to keep him from roaming at night. He had had forty stitches in his head by the age of three, because he kept climbing and falling–out of trees, off roofs. At six, he came home from school by walking along the roofs of houses.

It was virtually impossible to ride with Timmy in the car. He would lean halfway out an open window or climb all over the driver. He could not be controlled in such public places as restaurants or supermarkets.

"All I wanted was someone to help this child," said Mrs. Anderson. "All I seemed to do was take him to the hospital emergency room or go to the school humiliated to apologize for something he had done. The principal said, 'Smack him on the rear.' She didn't know we had beaten this boy practically unconscious. The teacher said, 'Make him do his homework.' I sat with him for two or three hours every night, slapping him most of the time because he couldn't do the work. One evening I found myself about to slam his head against the wall.

"School personnel said Timmy was disturbed or retarded. His first-grade teacher once asked me, 'Wouldn't you be satisfied if he could just learn to recognize that exit sign over there?'"

Timmy never finished his beginning reader. The first signs of pressure caused him to fall apart. He would not recite in front of the class. He crawled under his desk in school one morning and told his teacher, "Call the policemen and the firemen. Me not gonna read."

"I reached the point where I could no longer control my rages," said Mrs. Anderson. "I had total feelings of failure. He upset our whole life. While talking to my husband one night I found myself jumping out of the chair and screaming, 'I hate him! I hate him!'"

When Timmy entered the state institution for the emotionally disturbed, at the age of six, his family felt "overwhelming relief" at his removal from their care—and then immediate guilt for feeling good. Yet four years there brought only regression. He still could not read or write. His temper tantrums had increased markedly. Then a new psychologist at the institution suggested that Timmy be taken for testing at a private school designed for children with learning disabilities. That was where, at the age of ten, his disability was discovered.

Timmy's handicap, believed to have been caused by momentary deprivation of oxygen during birth, made it extremely difficult for him to translate his thoughts into words. He had a limited stock of words to choose from, and those were words that referred only to things he could see or feel. He had virtually no vocabulary with which to express his desires and emotions. He burned with rage because he could not say what he was thinking. It was so much easier for him to do things than to speak that he used whirlwind activity to make up for his skimpy vocabulary. Asked why he played with matches, he said, "Don't make me. Shut up! I'll kill you dead!"

Timmy was enrolled in the private school. He was given intensive training to expand his vocabulary and help him express his thoughts in organized language. Medication calmed his behavior and allowed him to concentrate on his schoolwork. He began to learn, to climb past the second-grade level at which he had been mired. In six months, aided by the medication and the fact that he was learning at last, Timmy's gross misbehavior eased. He started to read for pleasure for the first time in his life. He enjoyed school and became a good student. He learned to accept and use constructive criticism, instead of exploding whenever it was offered.

In three years of hard work, he pulled up to his proper grade level. His IQ, which had been in the dull-normal area, moved well into the normal range. Timmy graduated from twelfth grade in the private school. He is now in junior college studying accounting and will probably transfer to a four-year college.

Timmy overcame most of his learning disabilities, far beyond his parents' expectations. He illustrates how many learning-disabled children can be helped to virtual normality.

"Each gain that Timmy makes is measured from the last step," his mother told the author. "He is always surprising us in being able to accomplish tasks or reach levels we would never have expected of him. Our attitude toward him is almost the same now as toward our normal children. Our goal, of course, is to help him be self-sufficient and employable and married. And why not? We never thought he'd ride a two-wheeler, or be able to travel confidently to and from New York City alone, or even be able to multiply numbers. That last took him ten years to accomplish."

Mike's parents became aware early that he was different. He never liked the toys most children gravitate to. He showed very little curiosity. As he grew, he remained listless and played aimlessly if he played at all. When Mike was thirteen months old, his pediatrician suggested a neurological examination. The neurologist looked at Mike quickly ("Who can evaluate a human being in twenty minutes?" his mother was later to ask) and said, "Madam, you have a severely retarded son. He belongs in an institution for the rest of his life." In panic, the family consulted another neurologist; he told them Mike was mildly retarded. A third neurologist said nothing at all was wrong. Repeated physical examinations found him healthy.

Mike remained listless through his preschool years. When he was five, he entered a public-school kindergarten for retarded children. The next three years changed a quiet, sweet boy into a cranky, irritable child. He did nothing that first year but scribble endlessly with crayons. His attention span was dreadfully short. Was he in fact retarded? His parents began to wonder.

Midway through the year, a school psychologist told Mike's mother that her son was emotionally disturbed, not retarded, and should be transferred to a class for the emotionally disturbed. The psychologist also suggested counseling for Mike and his parents at a mental-health clinic in their rural eastern community. But a year of therapy achieved nothing.

Mike could not learn the alphabet in first grade, but he memorized a hundred words in his reading book and "read" to his teacher. He refused to try anything he did not think he could do. The other children were soon calling him "retard," and he began to balk at going to school. Yet his teacher passed him in every subject. "There seems to be a tendency in the schools when you get a child like this to just slide him through," Mike's mother said later. "Don't make waves."

Mike drifted through the first grades. Periodically he became so frustrated that he would pick fights in the classroom. He began to lie and to play with matches.

"No one gave us any help," Mike's mother recalled. "No one even tried. Who *was* he? What kind of child? Was he retarded? Was he disturbed? The professionals dumped the questions in our lap and walked away. They don't seem to care or to want to commit themselves. Unless the child disrupts the class. Then *you* fix him or take him out."

When Mike was eleven, his father was transferred to a large city in a mid-Atlantic state, and Mike was placed with his age group in a regular fifth-grade class. His new teacher immediately realized he could not work at that level. She suggested an examination by a pediatric neurologist, a specialist in neurological disorders of children.

This specialist was the first doctor to identify Mike's problem as learning disabilities combined with petit-mal episodes. Petit mal is a form of epilepsy in which the person who has it blanks out for a few seconds at a time. This accounted for Mike's lack of curiosity, his listlessness, and his seeming to tune people out.

Mike's learning disabilities were varied. He had a perceptual problem. All printed material was a blur to him, in spite of his normal vision; everything also appeared upside down or reversed. So he could not decipher a printed page. Basic number concepts threw him. He could not tell if the number of blocks in one pile was more or less than the number of blocks in another pile. He could not hold up two fingers when asked, or say how many pieces he would have if he cut an apple in half. Mike could not work well with his hands. A relative lack of control over his small muscles hampered his ability to draw and to write.

"Obviously, being unable to learn in an ordinary fashion, school provided a very frustrating situation for him and this would account for some of his behavior problems in school," the physician's report noted. "The only way Mike can be helped is to have intensive teaching assistance given by a person specially trained in working with learning-impaired children. If this help cannot be obtained for him, he cannot be expected to make any further progress in school."

Mike, too, was enrolled in a private school for learning-disabled children. His education began again at the beginning, with much of his time spent in individual training with specialists in perception and co-ordination. They helped untangle the scrambled way he saw letters and numbers. Work with concrete teaching aids, like rods of various lengths and colors, dramatically improved his ideas about quantity, and hence his arithmetic ability. He had to learn the difference between up and down, between near and far, in relation to his own body. He was given carefully guided exercises to develop efficient co-ordination between his hands and his eyes. Medication ended his petit-mal seizures.

"For the first time, things were explained to us," his father said. "Now we could work together. When he reverses letters on his homework, I don't holler, 'Concentrate!' I know it's not his fault. The rural school never told us he had a special problem. I had seen his letter reversals, but I didn't know what they meant."

In two years, Mike was up to fifth-grade work, and eventually he reached a level only one year behind children his own age. His chronic frustration and irritability disappeared. He became alive and alert.

Mike is a success—academically, emotionally, and socially. His IQ has more than doubled, jumping from what is considered to be retardation into the high-normal area. He has made his greatest gains in mathematics, mastering all the basic number concepts that had once baffled him. He has changed from a passive, tightly inhibited child into an outgoing and spontaneous teen-ager.

"Problems still exist," his mother reports. "Understanding his offbeat thinking. He is fascinated with matches; he seems to have enough sense to light them in the bathroom or in an open field, but still not enough not to light them at all. He is still not able to think all things out—lack of logic and common sense in so many areas, and yet so clever. But the progress! My Lord, he's a whole boy now, and the problems are slowly falling away.

"I keep wondering what if we hadn't moved? Would he still be shuttling between classes for the retarded and the disturbed?"

Jeannie had always seemed different from her brother, Dan. He was a placid boy, easy to raise and care for. She fussed and fumed and was miserably unhappy just about all the time. She seemed healthy, and her pediatrician couldn't be sure why she was such an uneasy child.

By the time Jeannie was two and a half, she was wild and uncontrollable. Her mother's nerves were worn trying to keep up with her and keep her out of trouble. Jeannie interfered with any kind of normal family routine. She fought with her brother because she wanted everything he played with. There seemed to be no way to make her content. She acted on every impulse, running, handling, grabbing, shouting. Neither parent could discipline her effectively. Patience simply seemed to stimulate Jeannie to even more outrageous behavior— demanding, crying, insisting on her own way. Spanking and yelling whipped the child into a frenzy of screams, kicks, and wild thrashing.

Life was torment for Jeannie's parents and obviously yielded no satisfaction to the child, either. Her parents were sensible enough to recognize that Jeannie was not deliberately bringing grief upon herself. They asked their pediatrician to check her closely. But he could not explain her uncontrollable behavior and referred Jeannie to a specialist, a pediatric neurologist at a nearby metropolitan medical center. The pediatric neurologist, Dr. Nathan, spent a lot of time with Jeannie. He saw her twice and then met with her parents. He told them that Jeannie had a neurologic impairment.

"It really doesn't matter too much what caused her condition," he explained to the parents. "The important thing is to understand that Jeannie has it, and that because of the impairment she can't control her behavior, or act and develop like other children.

"She's been so uncontrolled and impulsive that you probably aren't aware that her muscular co-ordination is not what it should be. Her speech development also is delayed. I'm going to set up a program to help Jeannie with her development. I will follow her on a regular basis until she is well along in school. I can't predict if she will have learning problems in school, but it seems likely. If we work carefully, we can help prevent learning problems from being too great, or from occurring at all. I'm pleased that you are meeting this problem early. It's much easier to help children like Jeannie—and the outcome is much more satisfactory—if we can find them while they are quite young."

Dr. Nathan wanted to calm Jeannie. He prescribed a mild medication. The medication did not "drug" her in any way. She reacted favorably within two weeks by seeming more calm and satisfied. She stopped charging around the house and became far less impulsive. She improved to the point where she was able to enter nursery school at the age of four. She did well, although her nursery-school teacher said Jeannie had a low frustration tolerance and became angry under any kind of stress. Jeannie also had a difficult time making her hands do what she wanted them to. It was hard for her to work on puzzles, to color within lines, to handle a pair of scissors.

Dr. Nathan recommended training with a co-ordination specialist, in this case an occupational therapist who specialized in working with children who had some form of mild neurological handicap. Jeannie enjoyed going to the co-ordination specialist for perceptual-motor training. She thought it was all a game and was delighted by her growing ability to handle crayons and pencils and to make things like scissors work properly.

The pediatric neurologist then suggested a psychological examination. A number of tests revealed that Jeannie had better-than-average intelligence, but confirmed a mild neurological impairment that was interfering with her development of muscular skills and language.

Other children seemed to understand what Jeannie was saying; but she did not make her sounds distinctly. The psychologist and Dr. Nathan suggested speech therapy, to try to avoid problems in kindergarten and beyond. A speech clinician began to see Jeannie and worked with her all through her kindergarten year.

By the age of six, Jeannie had improved so much with her co-ordination that the occupational therapist said no further perceptual-motor exercises were necessary. Jeannie's personality was changing as well. She was social and outgoing in kindergarten. She co-operated with the speech therapist and did all the exercises at home that were intended to overcome her improper pronunciation of some sounds.

Jeannie's kindergarten teacher thought she was still behind her classmates in some activities and wondered if Jeannie was ready for first grade at the age of six. Fortunately her birthday was in January, so Jeannie was older than most entering first-graders.

By now, Dr. Nathan was sure Jeannie could control herself without the need for medication. He first reduced the dosage and then eliminated the medication as Jeannie continued to show normal behavior and self-control. The speech clinician reported that Jeannie seemed to be making many of her sounds correctly, but thought she should continue with the child through first grade.

In first grade, Jeannie had minor problems starting to write, because her muscular control was not yet what it should have been. She had trouble staying within lines and making neat, legible letters. She was lucky that an expert learning-disability specialist was available in her public-school district. Jeannie's first-grade teacher asked this specialist to test the girl in visual perception and co-ordination and to prescribe a writing program for her. This worked, and Jeannie began to make progress.

She also had difficulty with beginning numbers work. The specialist thought that Jeannie needed help there as well. She took Jeannie out of class and worked with her alone for one period each week. Jeannie had trouble visualizing what numbers on a printed page meant. When she could *see* and *hold* a half-dozen pegs, she was aware that they meant *six*, which was one more than five but one less than seven and a lot less than ten. She could handle and manipulate these pegs and see for herself that two piles of six pegs made a total of twelve. She quickly learned that this meant the same thing as a dozen. After four months, Jeannie passed the need for concrete number aids and began to learn to use numerical principles.

School became a source of satisfaction to Jeannie. Bright and ambitious, she was eager to learn. She took advantage of all the help given her. Near the end of first grade, the speech clinician found that Jeannie was fairly normal in her speech and that there was no interference with her reading. The learning-disability specialist said Jeannie was up to grade level in arithmetic and writing. Dr. Nathan reevaluated her, and saw for himself that she had had a successful first year in school and seemed to need no further attention from him or the psychologist.

Jeannie was promoted. She was among the brightest pupils in second grade–with no sign that she had had difficulty or had made a slow beginning. She developed self-confidence. By the time she was ten, there wasn't the slightest trace of the difficulties that had made her early life a nightmare. Early attention from learning-disability specialists had solved her problems.

END

The Child at Home

Dear Mr. and Mrs. Brown:

We left too many things unsaid when you were in the office the other day. Let's discuss them.

We've examined Billy and believe he will do well in the new program his school has designed for him. Unfortunately, it's impossible to be explicit concerning the why and how of his learning disability. None of us know enough yet about children like Billy to tell you exactly what's happening and what to do about it. We wish we could say, "Oh, yes, it's blankitis, and a few shots of blankillin ought to clear it up."

We'd like to ease your anxiety. You are loving, caring parents. You have done a fine job raising your two older children. Then along came Billy, and all hell broke loose.

You know that Billy, like all other children, has certain basic needs. You are doing your best to satisfy them. You provide comfort within a close, tightly knit home. You see that Billy is kept safe from danger, well nourished, healthy. Because you want to provide the best care you can, you've had expert professionals analyze his behavior and his learning characteristics. They helped you make decisions concerning his education and medical treatment. But they told you little about handling the painful, upsetting problems that haunt you daily. Just where you need help the most—in your home life—you feel lost.

The methods you used with your other children don't work with Billy. Maybe your first two children had nap schedules that gave you, Mrs. Brown, time to yourself while they recovered a bit from their fussiness. But Billy was always wound up and jumpy when he should have been sleepy. You couldn't get him down to rest, and you couldn't get away from him to find a moment's peace. Your other two children quickly learned to hang up their clothes neatly. Billy scatters his pell-mell around his room. You have the devil's own time getting him to breakfast, while his brother and sister appear promptly and clean. You wonder if you are to blame. It occurs to you that if somehow you were only a little bit smarter you could handle Billy better. Your distress increases when grandparents or family friends, who mean well, suggest you are spoiling the boy, that you don't know how to handle him properly. Society's judgment in these matters is usually criticism of the parents—what could be easier? This is galling, because you know that Billy was different from birth.

Both of you will have to tread a fine line with Billy. He will absorb more than his share of your energy. Yet try as much as possible to give time and love to the rest of the family. Your other children can take an amazing amount of "benign neglect" if they understand *why* you have to devote so much of yourself to Billy and if they are offered assurance that their time will come as well. Plan activities with them alone. Handled right, Billy's brother and sister could be of great help. But not if they resent the child who seems to get most of the love and attention. Most youngsters behave with remarkable awareness and compassion if the emotional climate within their family is good and if their parents have a wholesome attitude toward themselves and their children, including the child with the problem.

Don't get so caught up in Billy's care that you lose outside interests. Keep up an active social life. Involve yourselves in recreation and community affairs. Try to relinquish his care periodically to a competent babysitter. It might be extremely hard to find a sitter who can handle and be trusted with a learning-disabled child. But attempt to find one who will learn, with encouragement and help, to stay with your child. You might trade time with the parents of other learning-disabled children. Both of you need the independence and the morale boost that will come from taking some time off, especially if you can go on vacation—even a long weekend—without any of your children. In sharing Billy's care, you'll free yourselves from the feeling of confinement and the ill effects of the tension and resentment that will inevitably build up if you alone are responsible for him.

Interpret his needs not only to people like babysitters or friends who come in briefly to pinch-hit for you, but also to your neighbors and relatives. Take the time and patience to try to help them understand Billy's problems. Most will gradually lose their apprehension about him and treat him as they do any child his age.

Keep channels of communication open within the family. Fathers sometimes play down problems and think their wives are unduly nervous. They come home from the office and are incredulous to be faced by an exhausted and now angelic child who, they are told, was raising hell earlier. A man may turn against his wife and berate her, because he believes he can control the child and his wife can't. Arguments can rise to bitter proportions.

SHE: You're not alone with him all day. It's fine for you in your air-conditioned office. I have to struggle with the laundry and the cleaning with this nagging brat hanging on me.

HE: If you think I'm going to put up with this after a busy day, you're crazy. What is this nonsense you're giving me about the kid's yelling and screaming in the supermarket? You let him get away with it. If you give in to him, he'll get a lot of satisfaction out of screaming his head off.

SHE: Just once I'd like to see you try to stop him when he takes it into his mind to go amok. He'd soon have you running back to your office.

So it goes. Parents must talk with each other, try to see each other's point of view, and respect each other's efforts to help the child. Instead of pulling in different directions, you must try to work together in your joint responsibility.

Our tests show us that Billy is bright and healthy, but his physical co-ordination makes him clumsier and his rate of language development has been slower than those of most children his age. He couldn't handle play tools in kindergarten and was lost with written symbols in first grade. But there were many other things Billy could do—until he decided to quit trying anything, because he had become convinced he was dumb.

Both of you are crushed by his school problems. You appear to take his difficulties personally, as affronts against you and your family. You believe that whatever he does reflects on you. You consider Billy—probably all your children—to be an extension of yourselves; by this reasoning, Billy's failures are your failures. So many parents feel this way. What a mistake and what a waste this is.

Our children are not extensions of ourselves. Unfortunately, in our society the achieving child is the ultimate status symbol. Perhaps it's because he is the only thing left we can't buy on time. When we think of our child as an extension—reflection—of ourselves, we put him in relentless competition for *our* rewards, the achievement of *our* victories, and we call the plays, whether or not he's ready or able.

Why did you both reject the kindergarten teacher's advice to hold Billy out of first grade for one year? For his sake, or because it might have reflected poorly on you or been awkward to explain to your family and friends? Mr. Brown, how could this possibly have been such a blow to your pride? You're a success in your business; you weren't going to be held back. Mrs. Brown, were you worried about Billy's feelings or your own? Children are innately honest little realists. Billy knew he couldn't do the work. He didn't need or want sympathy or excuses. All he wanted was someone to help him in a way that was right for him.

So often we try to rush nature, to push our children into activities for which they're not ready. We try to make them fit into a mold of our design, not theirs. This leaves them with little recourse. They can try halfheartedly to please us, really to get us off their backs; they can rebel, actively or by passive resistance; or they can just quit—withdraw into a world of daydreams. Children can develop many deviant behavior patterns as a reaction to pressures at home or in school, but in so doing their valuable constructive energies are dissipated. Learning becomes no longer a source of joyful discovery and mastery, but a painful striving to meet arbitrary, often inappropriate standards imposed by the adult world. Many children under stress begin to hate school, and they dawdle—sometimes actually get sick—in the morning so they can avoid it. At home, their inability to cope leads to excessive dependency, fearfulness, disobedience, and painful feelings of inferiority. Billy has tried many of these reactions.

They are the wrong reactions, but the best he can do under the circumstances. School and home are inseparable. Problems in one spill over into the other. If a child can't handle his classroom work, he's likely to be nasty and irritable when he is with his family. Unless he feels secure and believed in at home, he's likely to blow up when he gets to the classroom. All children are learning something every waking minute.

Billy has learned, with conviction, "I can't." His life (school and home) has taught him: You don't just *feel* inferior; you *are* inferior. You're a failure, a disappointment to everyone around you.

All children have abilities. These must be found; each youngster must be made aware of them. "Every child," says psychologist Gardner Murphy, in his book *Personality,* "is in some ways like all other children. In some ways he is like some other children. And in some ways, he is like no other child." Parents must look objectively at their children, see them as they truly are. In what ways is Billy like all children—with the same qualities and needs? What characteristics does he share with other learning-disabled children? And what are his unique personal strengths and weaknesses, the things you need to understand and work with?

The two of you must approach these questions together. You share the responsibility for helping Billy to solve his special learning and behavior problems. Your son will be far better off if he can't exploit rifts between his parents. You must create a favorable atmosphere within your home for seeking and finding ways to handle the tantrums and sulking that will occur. You will have to find ways to weave Billy into your family life; his management cannot be farmed out to a school or doctor.

His problems and behavior can't be viewed apart from your reactions—and those of relatives and friends—to him. He can't bear alone the burden of "causing all the trouble" in the household. For every action of his, there is a reaction. The reaction can aggravate the problem. Or it can reduce and correct it. "A barometer of human emotion, [this] child is unusually sensitive to parental feelings," a mother writes, in the newsletter of the California Association for Neurologically Handicapped Children. "If you cannot remain calm when he is disrupting the household, he will sense your feelings immediately and his own disruptive behavior will get worse. Strive for some objectivity, for [this child] needs your stability when he can't control himself. A good question to ask yourself is when does his behavior stop and your reaction begin?"

If you're truly objective, you won't let yourselves be beguiled by the notion that Billy's behavior is merely a phase he's going through. If you think—as some people will assure you—that it's merely a stage he'll grow out of, you will be inclined to procrastinate. You will not think of taking action to resolve his problems. Uncorrected, Billy could continue to pile bad behavior on bad behavior; this poor behavior might then harden into habits that will become more and more difficult to uproot.

Being objective means being realistic. Both of you must examine carefully the areas inwhich Billy does need help. Like many learning-disabled children, Billy in effect has to be taught how to live. You can't assume that he will pick up the basic rules of life by himself. You might have to spell things out for him. For example, you should see to it that he gets off to school well fed and appropriately dressed—comfortable with himself. You might have to ask him daily quite specifically—and as kindly as possible—whether he has brushed his teeth, washed his face and hands. You might have to remind him that the seasons have changed and it's now a wintry rather than an autumn day, so he ought to wear warmer clothing.

If you get to know his uniqueness as an individual, you'll also be aware of many tasks in which he is competent. Insist that Billy do the things you know he can do. You have seen him cut his meat at dinner, so don't do it for him. He can sweep with a push broom; assign him the job of keeping the garage and sidewalks clean. Gradually withdraw help as his need for it decreases, so he can assume greater initiative and self-reliance. Parents become so emotionally lopsided in the way they think about their learning-disabled children that they forget they must continually re-evaluate and try to take a fresh look at their youngsters. Parents frequently remain pessimistic, because all they think about is what's wrong with their child—never what's right. Billy is not helpless. Don't anticipate helpless behavior. Expecting his continued ineptness or difficult behavior will not make it more pleasant to tolerate—and he will act the way you expect him to act. Your other children will be quick to point out that you're applying different standards to Billy than you are to them. This can lead to resentment and quarreling.

Be alert to any hint that Billy is good at *something*, even at this early age. The discovery of areas of unimpaired ability, often of considerable native talent, allows the parents of learning-disabled children to give their youngsters new and venturesome chances for success. They need these opportunities. Don't impose your value standards. Don't be too quick to label genuine talents trivial or foolish. If Billy begins to show a talent for fly casting, for example, encourage it. Be enthusiastic if he decides he likes to cook. Whatever it is, be proud and support it. If you expose him to a wide variety of experiences, something *will* capture his interest.

Listen to what he says. Have an open mind. Don't step in and help him unless you're sure he can't do something alone. If he is always helped, if your impatient, quick, more able hands deny him the chance to try, he won't ever learn to master things for himself. This seems obvious, yet parents of learning-disabled children often are stunned when they are told they have overlooked abilities their youngsters have.

Don't worry about immediate usefulness. One learning-disabled twelve-year-old who had such poor co-ordination that he couldn't write very well started practicing magic. Inexplicably, he became a master at sleight of hand. His parents frowned on the pursuit, considering it an intrusion on his "more important" schoolwork. But magic was what this boy wanted to do. He also needed it to gain a feeling of importance and to fulfill a latent talent for showmanship. When he performed tricks that mystified his classmates, he gained a sense of satisfaction he could get no other way. His parents were persuaded by an understanding psychologist to buy him equipment and to take him to magicians' conventions. He began to earn money giving magic shows at parties and school assemblies. In time his co-ordination, which hadn't developed even after years of training in a special school, began to sharpen to an incredible degree, and the improvement carried over into writing, typing, and woodworking. Magic had become a worth-while pursuit in its own right, as an ego-building outlet; and ultimately it brought the boy an important return in the academic area.

Encouraged to do things in which he can succeed, no matter what they are, the learning-disabled child will discover self-respect. Find every conceivable way to help Billy learn that he can be successful. "The real remedial work for a child with a learning disability goes on at home," writes Mrs. Margaret Golick, a psychologist at Montreal Children's

Hospital, in *A Parents' Guide to Learning Problems*. Parents are the most important guide this or any child can have. Not in academic instruction. But you can work side by side with Billy in areas that intrigue him: the care of animals, model building, appliance repair. You can go fishing or camping with him. You can help him learn to swim, to dance. Many parents of learning-disabled children have become masters at finding ways to provide rewarding and productive day-to-day learning experiences for their children.

"Only the home can provide the variety, the repetition, the relevance that [this child] needs," Mrs. Golick says. "Parents can make mealtime, bedtime, a drive in the car, a trip to the supermarket and ordinary household activities into meaningful teaching situations.... If mother or father takes the trouble to teach systematically some of the skills involved in cleaning, cooking, shopping, gardening, there is an ideal opportunity to develop finger dexterity, visual and auditory perception; to teach order, logic, arithmetic; to sharpen a child's ability to use language.... Involvement in the life of the household gives a feeling of competence that can help to counteract the sense of failure instilled by low marks."

(Parenthetically, there is rarely a parent, even one who is a good teacher of academic subjects for other children, who can be effective tutoring his or her own youngster. Parents are too emotionally involved with their children to be objective. When the mother-child relationship, or the father-child, is converted to that of teacher-child, the child in effect no longer has a mother, or a father, but only one more mediocre teacher. Yet so fixed is present-day society's lunatic demand for academic excellence that the minute a child starts to experience failure in first grade, his parents sweep in to tutor him. This usually is the beginning of misery for both parents and child.)

Parents help most when they know what a child can and cannot do. Encourage Billy to work only on tasks he can accomplish. There are a number of assignments suitable for him around the house, if you'll only think. They can be as simple a part of family living as folding napkins, setting the table, or helping with a minor kitchen chore like shelling peas. These give the child a feeling of success, and they are also helpful exercises for eye-hand co-ordination. If Billy makes a mistake, he need not incur anyone's wrath. Learning to hang laundry on a line could be a helpful activity for him if you don't insist that the clothespins be placed exactly at the seams or if you can bear to see things rumpled while he figures out a way to get them across the line.

If Billy fails at a job you've given him, it might be because you have expected too much. Find challenges that are within his abilities. If you match tasks to his level of functioning, Billy will succeed. And if you've paved the way with easy-to-wipe-clean surfaces and break-proof containers, for example, spills will fade in importance compared to the newly learned co-ordinative skill involved in concocting a salad. Montessori books, available in your local library, detail a number of jobs for children that you can easily adapt to your home. (These are Dr. Maria Montessori's "exercises in practical life.")

No child should feel he's being pressured to learn something every minute of the day. But, comfortably and consistently in his daily life, Billy should get a happy feeling that he is helping at home, handling things well, and having fun. All children, but especially learning-disabled boys and girls, learn best by practice in real situations. No lecture will be as effective as a demonstration of the activity itself–and then letting him do it lots of times.

Parents differ in their standards for doing a job right, so you should decide beforehand how strongly you feel about results. Reward any honest effort that is in the direction of the desired result. Children who are clumsy learn much more when they are free of pressure and criticism.

Too many parents get irritated by children who do their best and still get things wrong. Why should Billy try to hang up his trousers if, after he does so, you criticize him because he's done a sloppy job? He's trying, and he's getting there little by little. That deserves praise. Mothers get too impatient with fumbles in household routines, or when a child puts his shoes on the wrong feet and cannot tie his laces. Fathers become disappointed and impatient if their children are not good at sports or working with tools.

Think about *his* problems. Can you figure out something that will help Billy put his shoes on correctly? Perhaps you could draw outlines of his shoes on the closet floor and indicate which is left and which is right. Or could you mark the inside of the shoes with pictures to show where the big toe goes?

Mrs. Brown, you're concerned because Billy doesn't listen, can't remember his lessons, forgets his lunch money, dawdles over dressing and eating. We discussed this dependency—for that's exactly what it is—because it irritates your husband to see you "baby the boy." Billy is overly dependent on you. You're much more protective of him than of your older children. Because of his handicap, his slowness and clumsiness in learning how to take care of himself physically, you bathed, fed, and dressed him long after you needed to. Your concern leads you to respond to Billy's whims instead of to his needs. Parents who do this, who give in at every turn, add to their children's problems. They cause their youngsters to regress, to become more, rather than less, infantile.

Billy can't stand up for himself. You feel sorry for him and fight his battles. He has learned to rely on you, to exploit you to get everything he wants without effort on his part. So he stands in his own way in developing independence. And you, like so many loving mothers, have become enslaved by the chains of dependency you helped forge. Listen to your husband when he says, "Let him do it himself." Try to develop some of his detachment. Fathers seem to understand the laws of cause and effect better than mothers do. Mr. Brown is legitimately concerned every time you allow Billy to miss school or get out of doing his homework because he has complained of a headache or that his stomach hurts. Mr. Brown lives in a real world; nobody in his office cares whether he's got a headache, as long as he produces his work. He feels, rightfully, that Billy has to learn this way of the world. He expects Billy to grow up to be a productive citizen and knows the boy must start learning to produce now. But Billy thinks his mother has given him a free ride.

Learning-disabled youngsters need firmness, consistency, and clarity more than other children do. "Routine is to a child what walls are to a house," psychiatrist Rudolf Dreikurs and Vicki Soltz write, in *Children: The Challenge*. "It gives boundaries and dimensions to his life." This is true for all children, but especially for youngsters like Billy. You have described the quarrel you had because Mrs. Brown let Billy miss school one day so he could sleep late. Mr. Brown had come in from a trip the night before, and Billy had been allowed to stay up past his bedtime to greet his father. He slept late the next morning. Mrs. Brown, you even wrote a note to Billy's teacher saying he hadn't been well. You were hurt and angry because Mr. Brown criticized you for letting Billy skip school and for writing that note. By allowing Billy to stay up late, you denied him his right to attend to his own business the next day, and you interfered with his right to proper rest. It also ruined the next day for all of you, because Billy was even more active and disorderly than usual. The false excuse you wrote to the school told Billy that lies could be used to avoid unpleasant consequences.

Like all children, Billy will test limits. He'll try to see how far he can go. If he finds no boundaries, he'll become confused and will demand more and more license to do as he pleases. When someone finally clamps down on him, he won't know what hit him, and he might erupt like Vesuvius. Be sure Billy knows what you expect, the rules of the house. Tell him what the consequences will be if he does not obey the rules. Always follow through. Don't let yourself be swayed by his wiles. If a child senses his parents are wavering, he could provoke them to criticize each other in front of him. Try not to let this happen. Help Billy realize that he is responsible to both parents equally. But be sure he understands the rules and the penalties for infractions.

Not long ago we were stopped by a policeman, for speeding. The policeman politely handed out a ticket. With equal grace the judge accepted payment of the fine. Neither the policeman nor anyone in the traffic court yelled or nagged. The law was understood; there had been signs along the road to remind drivers of the speed limit. The author knew he was violating the law. The penalty was also known, and it was administered quietly, without scorn, without anger. Thus does everyone learn effectively that he has to pay for his actions. The penalty for speeding was paid in the same way that Billy must calmly and emotionlessly be brought to account for poor behavior. Calmly and deliberately, without rancor, without humiliating criticism, without derision.

Many adults who pride themselves on being loving parents somehow don't see anything wrong in mocking or teasing their children. They are surprised when told that their teasing is a harsher punishment than any honest beating they might administer. Somehow people believe scorn and derision don't hurt children. "But it was just a joke," some will say. Derision is not funny. The fact that you are criticizing with laughter makes the criticism more scathing to youngsters, who would rather you told them straight out that you are angry—and why.

This doesn't mean you should not get angry. Try to deal with Billy as calmly as possible. But everyone is driven to angry outbursts at times. Express your anger honestly and directly: "I'm *damn* mad. You know I won't stand for your using my tools without asking. I looked all over for the wrench when the toilet wouldn't flush. And now I find it, two days later, lying in the grass and rusting. I'm furious, and you might as well know it."

Kindness and sympathy are essential, but they cannot take the place of firm, fair discipline for the learning-disabled child. When you punish, try to do it fairly and calmly—as the policeman did. "Punishment should be prompt," says pediatrician George W. Brown, in an article in the *Journal of Learning Disabilities*. "Delay causes the child to be confused about what he did wrong [and] gives the child a long period of worry and resentment that may be out of proportion to the situation. Let the punishment fit the crime. Do not impose a major punishment for a minor transgression. Don't punish the same behavior with widely different penalties at different times. Avoid long sermons, talk, logical reasoning. Make the handling of the problem direct and simple. Don't demand verbal assurances that he will never do such a thing again.... Try to avoid punishments that are violent or lead to great excitement. Don't let your own feelings of anger and frustration distort the situation into something it isn't.... Use punishments that involve withholding of privileges or putting the child in quiet isolation. Make clear to the child that you dislike his action, not him.... The child usually needs an improved self-image, not degradation. Avoid self-defeating threats, bribes, promises, and sermons. Politeness cannot be taught by ... harangues; bickering and harsh criticism are sometimes more inflammatory than instructive.... It is a mistake to be too strict and then too forgiving. Avoid cold anger at one time, then loving embraces soon after. Hold your temper if you want [your] child to learn that temper can be held."

A family must set up a structure, or routine, within which all members can live comfortably. Billy should have a regular time to get up every morning. Get him an alarm clock. Make out a timetable *with him* and pin it up in his room. Include time for play, homework, reading, television, going to bed, waking up, and meals.

He needs a list of chores, too. It doesn't matter whether you have a maid or Mrs. Brown is the maid. He can make his bed, clean his room, put away his own laundry, empty the trash, and run errands. He might not do these things as well as you would, but accept his efforts and express pleasure when he handles something particularly well. Don't rob him of his dignity by doing anything over again. Don't remake his bed. Never mind how it looks to others. Be pleased he got it together at all. You might even show him how to get it a little smoother next time.

Children need and love order. When rules and routines are established, they will live within them with a strong sense of security. And so will parents. There are times that rules or routines will have to be changed for good reason. But it must be made clear that those are exceptions, and are not just to satisfy parental or child whim.

Since you two are the authorities, the rules in your home will depend on your values and the kind of home you want. They should be based on the principles you have taught your children, the principles *you* live by and that your youngsters can understand and respect. Children who are taught to obey principles, rather than parental whim, are less often confused, rebellious, or misled by temptation. Be sure every member of your family understands the rules and the punishments for infractions.

Once you have set the rules, see that they are enforced evenhandedly. Don't let Billy badger one of you for an extension of bedtime when you both have already agreed what that time should be. Don't let him appeal to anyone else. Refuse to be drawn into a popularity contest with grandparents, for example. Be direct with them. Be sure they know they aren't doing Billy any good when they vie with you for his favor by being permissive toward him. You should also be able to check if your other children are complying with the rules. Rules are meaningless unless you can enforce them.

Physical punishment is rarely good. Physical restraint, presented to Billy as your way of helping him to control himself so that he won't hurt himself, is a better idea. One of the authors learned a valuable lesson some years ago from his work with a number of learning-disabled boys who were "wall climbers." Some of these boys had withstood every effort of their parents and professionals to calm them. They were defiant, aggressive, accustomed to having their own way. Their tantrums were ferocious. These youngsters had learned to control any situation they were in. The adults around them, fearful of setting off small riots, had refused to exert their authority. One day, in desperation, the author firmly and unemotionally placed one child face down on the floor and sat on him—astraddle on his buttocks. The boy screamed and thrashed wildly, but soon realized he was helpless in that position. The dead weight on his buttocks, unyielding to any entreaties, persuaded him that freedom would come only if his antics stopped. The technique worked. He, and others on whom this method was subsequently tried, could have their freedom—could rejoin the human race—only by quieting down. It was amazing how quickly they did.

It is hard for parents and teachers to handle this kind of youngster. Usually a method can be found, but parents often let up too soon, before a technique has had time to work. Professionals usually have to prevail upon parents to try a method long enough to allow it to take effect. So it's often wise to begin a program of behavior control under guidance. Professionals can be objective concerning goals, the extent to which the child's behavior is being improved, and how long a specific method of behavior control might be needed before it could reasonably be expected to help. You might need professional help to teach you to observe Billy, to define your goals for him, to identify what is acceptable behavior and what is not. More and more psychologists and special-education teachers are prepared to offer instruction in handling the behavior problems of learning-disabled children.

Whether their behavior is seriously out of control or not, most children, normal or learning-disabled, become more manageable when their parents are consistent with discipline. It is hard to be consistent, and virtually impossible to be so all the time. But few parents realize how uneven they are. Parents who talk with counselors about their disciplining efforts are often amazed to learn how many times what they *do* actually contradicts what they intend.

Children are keenly observant. They readily mimic what others do. The learning-disabled child is even more inclined to copy. Parents who contradict their discipline by their own actions will have major problems with a learning-disabled child. This boy or girl is most uncertain how to behave, and sometimes he is confused about the principles that are supposed to govern his behavior. However, he understands what he observes, and that is what he's going to use as a model for his actions. If you value a certain type of behavior, don't just talk it up; do it yourself. That's what Billy will learn. If you behave inconsistently, he will too.

The point applies to anything you tell him. There is no value in stressing the benefits of industriousness, for example, if Billy doesn't see you engaged in serious work. If you talk about learning as good for its own sake and he sees no evidence that you read books or discuss issues seriously, he will have no impulse toward valuing knowledge. If you decry materialism at the same time that you boast of each glittering new possession, Billy will sense that hard work is not necessarily its own reward and will expect to be paid off, as he thinks you are, for every effort he makes, for everything he learns. Set consistent, dependable models. Be sure there is no distance between what you practice and what you preach.

Keep your word. In the throes of a screaming tantrum at the shopping center, Billy once got you to placate him with "If you stop crying, I'll take you to the zoo Saturday." Billy stopped, Saturday came, and you did not take him to the zoo. He had been rotten all week long and didn't deserve to go. But you had made an explicit promise. You should not have said it unless you meant to carry it out.

When Billy behaves well, try giving him simple immediate rewards or use tokens—things like poker chips—that can be translated later into things that appeal to him. If his good behavior always earns him an instant reward, even if it is a piece of candy, he will see a direct benefit, one that will be forthcoming consistently. Promises are empty to children with learning disabilities. They refer to a far-off time. Both you and Billy are likely to forget. Billy can't learn to control himself in public that way. He *can* learn if he is given a poker chip—later to be traded for something he really values, perhaps an ice cream cone—each time he keeps himself quiet and under control on a trip to the supermarket. All parents properly reward their children for good behavior by recognition, praise, often a treat. Learning-disabled children need a reward that is as immediate and concrete as possible. You're not bribing the child; you're helping him to control his behavior and to understand that he will benefit directly from this self-control. In time he'll learn to control his behavior without immediate, concrete rewards.

Be wary of making threats. So many parents usher their children through stores—and childhood—with virtual nonstop commentary on the order of "If you touch the counter one more time, I'll smack you!" The youngster keeps grabbing everything on the counter, and nothing happens—just another empty threat that the child comes to dismiss scornfully. Often the clever youngster understands that his mother will carry out the threat only after six to eight warnings, so he's fairly safe the first five times. Or he can detect a rising intensity in his mother's voice with each repetition and knows at about what decibel level she'll carry out her threat. What Billy will learn is not respect for his parent's wishes, but that his parents may or may not mean what they say, and he will learn how to manipulate them. Don't threaten until you mean it. If you do threaten, fulfill the threat just as soon as Billy does the thing you have been warning him about.

Be direct in talking with your son. Don't be inveigled into tortuous explanations. Explain simply why his poor manners upset you. It doesn't make any sense to him when you say, "I just can't stand the way you act at dinnertime. I want you to be better behaved." It's much more understandable to spell it out: "The last time we had mashed potatoes I noticed that you tried to eat them with your knife. Tonight we're going to put just the mashed potatoes on your plate. I want to see you eat them with your fork."

Be brief; be clear. If you give an order be sure it's understood. Give the child time to follow through. Show your satisfaction. Then give the next instruction. Spell out what you expect in simple, easy terms. Try to be positive. Support and direct, rather than criticize. Avoid saying, "Billy acts like a baby, so we're treating him like one." Instead say, "Billy is learning to sit still at the table and eat his meal without a fuss." Give your instructions in a pleasant and encouraging tone of voice. Remember that Billy is not deliberately malicious. While his annoying behavior might be beyond his present control, you can eventually lead him, through your understanding, to learn to control himself better. A behavior pattern like Billy's is not immutable. He will mature and change.

Like many learning-disabled children, Billy frequently has difficulty following instructions. You won't always know if this is defiance or if he simply does not understand. Be as concrete as possible when you ask him to do something. One helpful technique is to phrase your directions simply, in short, terse sentences. Tell him, "Look at me while I speak." If you are not sure he understood, ask him to repeat what you said. If, in spite of his repetition, you still believe he doesn't know what you meant, ask him to demonstrate what you asked for.

Most of the behavior problems learning-disabled children have at home can be prevented by removing excessive stimulation and by making their activities as predictable as possible. Learn to anticipate what situations will be overstimulating to Billy. Keep those within simple, clear-cut limits. Overreaction to things that other children take in stride—a party, a picnic—need not be a fixed, unchangeable part of your youngster. A learning-disabled child's reaction can sometimes be altered if you clearly understand what causes it. Then you can modify the aspect of the family environment that triggers Billy's outbursts. For example, does having guests for dinner set him off? First, let him know in advance that company is coming. Then encourage him to stay in his room until the guests are assembled, because you understand that he becomes unnerved and overexcited by each new arrival.

Keep Billy's room simple and, if possible, in the quietest part of your home. It should be a retreat, a place in which he can relax. If he cannot have a room to himself, give him the part of a room that is farthest from the door and hallway, perhaps behind a folding screen. Keep as many of his possessions as you can on shelves in a closet. Few toys should be strewn about. As one mother suggests, modern laundry appliances enable most of these youngsters to get along with fewer sets of clothing, and therefore to benefit from less confusion over what to wear and from less of a visual jumble of clothing thrown about the room.

If you're not sure what activities overstimulate Billy, observe him carefully. It may be that activities do not bother him as much as his brother does, by picking on him incessantly. The two of them may have to be kept apart as much as possible. If you're not sure about cause, alter just one thing at a time and observe the effects carefully. Be sure you allow enough time for any behavior change to show.

Simplify family routine. Many children with learning disabilities are especially fussy and irritable at mealtime. Most people don't regard mealtime as anything out of the ordinary. But think how complex a situation it can be. Everyone in the family is talking. The table is laden with food; aromas assail the nostrils. The room is bustling with activity. There probably is teasing and banter. You think nothing of this, might even find it pleasant. Then everybody's serenity is shattered when Billy—unable to cope with all the sights, sounds, and smells—yells, kicks his brother, and throws his fork across the table.

If this happens, don't let the situation get overheated to the point that everyone becomes upset. Step in immediately and take charge. Give Billy an escape route. You might let him leave the table and sit at a small table off to one side of the room. He might have to sit by himself, with a pared-down table setting, for a while. When he can take that much stimulation, you might ask him to rejoin the family group for dessert. Give him some extra space at your table. Move him bit by bit into more difficult situations. At first he might still become overexcited by the talk at the dinner table, and all of you would have to control yourselves. If the dessert experiment is successful, let him rejoin you for a full meal. Perhaps by then he'll be able to juggle his food and a bit of conversation, too. Later he can share the experience of eating at a friend's home, and later still in a restaurant. Start with the simplest situations, and gradually introduce complexities as you believe Billy can take them. The goal is *to help him* join the family in as much of its routine as possible, as long as he can keep himself under control, enjoy a family experience, and not shatter the rest of the family.

If Billy gets seriously out of control and simplification of family activities doesn't do enough, you will have to consider other techniques. Try a "time-out" room. Tell Billy what kind of behavior you expect of him. Define what you will accept as good behavior and what you will punish with isolation. If he doesn't comply, calmly and unemotionally place him alone in any quiet room. You might have to restrain him to get him into this time-out room. In this case, pick him up firmly, without hysterics, and *move* him.

Billy is there to regain his composure, to settle down. Tell him he can rejoin the family as soon as he has himself under control. Combine use of the time-out room with rewards, praise, and support for his good behavior.

Billy doesn't play well with other children. He hasn't had much chance to learn. First, he can't keep up with them. Second, your excessive concern leads you to behave differently with him than with your other youngsters. You don't interfere with their squabbles; you don't try to protect them from getting hurt. Unlike Billy, they are learning to give as well as take, to know that other children have the same rights as they do.

Billy has to understand that he must live with other children in a world that doesn't revolve around him. Yet he still requires organized routine and help. Consider sending him to camp next summer. He will be nine–that's old enough. Don't worry about his wandering off or losing his shoes. He'll learn to keep track when no one is there to take care of things for him. Camp also will give him good training in physical coordination.

In the meantime, Mr. Brown, work with Billy on game skills. He can learn to succeed at some games, at first simple ones broken down into small component parts that will be easy for him to handle. Try to adapt some of these games to your home. Start with ones that don't demand the abilities he lacks. Gradually introduce others that require more and different kinds of skills. Card and board games come in all levels of difficulty, and with judicious selection you can gradually introduce concepts at higher and higher levels. Elements of popular games like baseball can be taught separately. There may be no hope for Billy's batting, but he can be helped to play an easy position in the field. First teach him to catch large, slow objects–yarn balls or balloons.

Build his confidence and interest so he will welcome being with other children, playing with them. He must feel he has something to contribute. This is extremely important. The most miserable child in school is not the one who can't learn to read, but the one who always loses the race, who can't handle a ball, who is never chosen to be on anybody's team–clumsy Billy, who needs him? He's miserable on the playground, because other children don't want him. You might be upset because Billy can't carry a glass of water, even one only half full, without spilling it. But your concern doesn't come near the agony that Billy must feel every day. (It's ironic that after a boy grows up nobody cares if he's clumsy. How many times have you asked your chairman of the board to play tetherball?) Parents often find that their learning-disabled children get involved in their worst quarrels during games they cannot play well. It's little wonder that many develop into poor losers. Be alert to help Billy *avoid* frustrating games in which he has no chance of success.

Every child needs to learn that he is significant. He will realize it only when he is treated with respect and allowed to do his own work–even if it's building a tower of blocks. His mother could say, "That's a great tower. Daddy will be home soon, and we'll save it to show him. As soon as you finish, it's time for your nap, dear." The child will learn to respect himself and his property, and this will, in turn, allow him to respect others and their property. Your Joe and Lisa have been gaining self-respect all along, but Billy hasn't, because others have usually completed his work for him or made excuses for him, instead of helping him to do things *in his way*, however slower and more awkward that is. He has not been allowed to learn that he can be master of his own actions. He can be, you know, but it will take more time and patience on the part of everyone in the family.

By now, perhaps you've begun to realize that much of your anger with each other has grown out of disagreements over Billy. Your son might not have caught on to reading, but he has learned to tyrannize the two of you. Remember when you canceled the trip to New York because of a fight over him? He had staged a tantrum and torn up some of the other children's toys. Mr. Brown, you punished him severely, and Mrs. Brown fell apart. Billy came downstairs calm and serene after his explosion to fix himself a glass of chocolate milk, but you two canceled a vacation and spent that time storing up more resentment against each other.

Support, encourage, and appreciate each other, so that Billy will be able to reflect this strengthening kind of love. Help him move gradually to independence, so he can maintain the dignity of childhood and the self-respect that comes with doing as much as possible for himself. Accept his contributions to the family, no matter how small, with appreciation and a genuine pleasure that he can recognize. Accept his individuality. It will be harder for Billy to learn to cope with many things, but with the patience and kindness that accompany your respect for him, you can find a way to teach him.

Be optimistic, be positive, but most of all help your child to help himself. Don't hinder him. He needs you. Your job is far more important than that of the teacher, the pediatrician, or the psychologist. Don't get discouraged; don't let up. Ultimately you will see the success of your efforts, as Billy develops talents and becomes independent and his own master. The greatest gift you can give Billy is to provide him with a home life that teaches him he is a valuable and responsible part of it, a contributing member of the family, loving and very lovable. He can learn these lessons *only* at home. And they are far more important than spelling, the multiplication tables, and learning how to print neatly.

END

From "Gifford on Courage"

Herb Score

It was Bob Feller all over again. A kid who could move from the dirt ballfield and splintered stands behind the high school gym right into the major leagues and take on Williams and Mantle and the rest on even terms. He had a fast ball that Yogi Berra called "unfair," a curve that broke almost at a right angle, and if he could only get his control into shape, why he was sure to win 20 games his first year and, lord, maybe into infinity.

His first trip—age 18—to meet the Cleveland brass might have been the wish of a Little Leaguer. "Just warm up, son, and we'll see what you have." The first few pitches crack into the catcher's mitt and a coach roars out of the dugout screaming, "I told you to take it easy; don't bear down until you're warm." And the apologetic response: "I'm not bearing down, sir." The catcher surreptitiously slips a sponge rubber pad into his glove.

We revel in new heroes, a fresh name to take its place beside Grove, Alexander, Johnson, Spahn in the pantheon of our memories. Young, skinny Herb Score seemed destined. Three fantastic years in succession, one in the highest rung of the minors, two in the majors. He wins 36 and loses 19 those two years with Cleveland. He strikes out 245 the first year and 263 the second. Both records. (Feller didn't strike out 240 until his third year; Grove, whom many call the best lefthander ever, until his sixth.) He wins Rookie of the Year in the minors and repeats the next year with Cleveland.

Then he's through. He doesn't have another winning season. In the baseball vernacular, he loses his arm.

Herb Score. Mention his name even to a marginal baseball fan and you'll hear, "Oh, yeah, he was the guy who was hit in the eye by McDougald's line drive. Shame. Great promise. Knocked him right out of baseball."

Did it? How *does* an arm go bad? When a spur begins to grow? When the chill of a spring night game subtly alters musculature? When a baseball traveling 130 miles an hour smashes into an eye? So much the magic of medicine can't tell us; along with the diseases that ravage man, why does a pitcher suddenly lose his arm?

Herbert Score, 41 and totally gray, sportscaster for the Indians, is doing some missionary work before a room jammed with members of the Napoleon, Ohio, Kiwanis Club (they even permitted a few eager wives in this night; but *after* dinner). Score speaks well, with a fine self-directed wit.

"During my first season with Cleveland, we made an early visit to New York where I was born. I was hoping to pitch against the Yankees. I figured I'd walk onto that field and every kid I'd gone to school with would be there and I'd show them what I'd become. But Al Lopez was a bright manager. He wasn't going to use me. It would be Early Wynn Friday night, Mike Garcia Saturday and Bob Lemon Sunday. Saturday afternoon, Lemon is running in the outfield and pulls a muscle in his leg. After the game Saturday, Lopez tells me, 'We don't know if Lemon's leg will be all right tomorrow. If he can't pitch, you're going to start against the Yankees. Get to bed early tonight.'

"Next morning it's Sunday and I decide to go to St. Patrick's Cathedral. I'm in there kneeling, praying. And as I'm meditating and praying, I said, 'Lord, Bob Lemon hurt his leg yesterday. They don't know how serious it is and he's been awfully nice to me, taken me to dinner. He's a great pitcher, won 20 games six or seven times and he's just an outstanding person. But if you could see your way clear he couldn't walk today, I'd appreciate it.'

"I get to the ballpark and they're still not sure if Lemon's going to be able to play, so they tell us both to warm up. If Lemon's leg doesn't hurt, he'll pitch. About 10 minutes go by and they decide he's okay and tell me to sit down. It's about time for the game to start and rather than run across the field to the bullpen, I decide to walk underneath the stadium concourse.

"I start out and I'm passing the concessions. You know, nothing smells as good as hot dogs at a ballpark. Absolutely nothing. I'm walking and I'm smelling. If I only had some money, I'd buy some hot dogs. In those days, I was always hungry. I strike up a conversation with a couple of fellows. Pretty soon I have two hot dogs. I keep walking and I hear the game start. At the head of the ramp going down to the bullpen, there's another concession stand. I thought, the hot dogs were good. A little ice cream to wash it down wouldn't be bad. Sure enough, another conversation; I end up with a box of ice cream.

"Sit down on the bench and by now the Yankees are at bat. I open my shirt, take off my cap, close my eyes and I'm ready to take a little sun. All of a sudden, I feel a tug at my sleeve and I open my eyes and there's Mel Harder, our pitching coach. He's pointing toward the mound. I see Lopez standing there waving his left hand. Harder says, 'I think he wants you.' And I say, 'That's what I'm afraid of.'

"I climb over the railing and start across the outfield toward the mound. Yankee Stadium, 60,000 people, something I've dreamed of since I was a kid and here I am gurgling with every step.

"Finally get to the mound, Lopez tells me Lemon's leg is hurting, the umpires realize this and I can take all the time I need to warm up. I figured it might take three days. But we get under way and it gets into the fifth or sixth inning and somehow the Yankees load the bases and there are no outs. I look up and here's Mickey Mantle at the plate. We all know there's a lot of criticism of baseball for being a long game, being too slow, and usually they blame the pitcher and they say how come he holds the ball so long. As long as I'm holding it, he can't hit it.

"I know I have to do something and then I hear someone call time out. Al Rosen's playing third base, sort of the unofficial team captain. He's called time and he's going to walk over and I know I'm going to get this wonderful piece of advice.

"Rosen calls the shortstop and they have a little meeting. Now

Rosen comes to the mound. He and the shortstop have worked it all out. 'Hey kid,' he says, 'you're really in trouble.'

"The mind is a wonderful thing and frequently we're able to forget unhappy events. I don't remember the details from that point, except learning why Mantle is paid all that salary, but I'm young and I'll have lots of chances at the Yankees and we continue to Boston.

"I had heard a lot about Ted Williams and I'm looking forward to pitching against him. So the first time we play the Red Sox, I'm geared up to face Williams. But he's not in the line-up. Has the flu. Two weeks later, we have another series with Boston. And again, I'm ready for Williams. Again, he's not in the line-up. A suspicion grows. Possibly Williams doesn't want to face Score. It's understandable. He's getting on—34, 35 years old—and his reflexes are shot and he possibly couldn't get around on a fast ball any more. I'd been having a good spring. Won a couple of games. I could understand his reluctance.

"It gets to be June and the Red Sox are in Cleveland. Finally, Williams is going to meet Score. I know this because they have it in the newspaper and they're never wrong. I could hardly wait to warm up. It's the first inning and here comes Williams, batting third. I'm not the kind of pitcher, incidentally, who looks back to see where his fielders are playing each batter. I didn't know where I was going to throw it, so I sure didn't know where they were going to hit it.

"But I notice suddenly that the team is shifting way over to the right, the Boudreau shift. The shortstop is on the right side of second base, the second baseman almost in right field, Rosen all alone on the left side of the infield. I was thinking, if I say anything to them, they'll think I'm a fresh rookie and I shouldn't talk, all those veteran ballplayers. There's no way Williams can pull me, not *my* fast ball, but I figure they'll find out for themselves. Count gets to be three balls and a strike and Williams hits a little fly ball into left centerfield.

"The Cleveland stadium sits out there on the lake and very unusual wind currents blow off the water. Somehow this ball gets up into one of those unusual currents and that lazy fly ball hits the fence 385 feet away. Williams has a double. I'm undaunted. He didn't *pull* the ball. When he comes up next time, I'll reach back, give it a little extra push

118

and zip right on by him. He comes up two innings later, I reach back for a little extra, he hits it into the upper deck in right field. In his first 16 times at bat, Williams hits four home runs, a double, and a single off me.

"So, next trip to Boston, Williams is in the line-up again. He's obviously regained his confidence as far as Score is concerned. Now I've rarely been able to get ahead of Williams. It's always two balls and no strikes, three balls and maybe one strike. I have two pitches, a fast ball and a curve, and the curve I usually don't get over. So if you want to guess what's coming, you have a pretty good percentage. I'd have Williams 3–0 and he'd say to himself, he's going to throw me a fast ball and I'm going to hit it 100 miles. And I'd say to myself, I'm going to throw him a fast ball and he's going to hit it 100 miles.

"But, now, I do get ahead of him. I get two strikes, no balls. I've got him. I've pitched a whole year and I know how to do this. I'm going to bounce the curve in front of home plate. Then I'm going to stomp around on the mound and kick some dirt and fume and Williams is going to say, ahah, he still can't get that curve over. Then I'm going to throw a fast ball right up under his chin. He's going to jump back and he's going to say, ahah, now he'll have to come in with a fast ball and then I'm going to throw the curve over the outside corner; he'll be so surprised he won't even swing, strike three. All figured out.

"I bounce the curve in front of the plate, stomp around, put on a pretty good show. Now I'm ready. Someone once told me it takes two-fifths of a second from the time a pitcher releases until the batter swings. You'd be amazed what goes through your mind in two-fifths of a second. I throw the ball. I see him start to swing. I notice he has a lovely swing. I see the ball over my head, and I think, boy, he sure didn't pull my pitch. I look back and all I can see is the centerfielder's number. I'm thinking, it carried pretty good, Larry Doby's going to have to hurry to catch it. Then I realize he's not going to catch it. He's going to play it off the wall in centerfield. Then I realize it's not going to hit the wall."

His audience warm, Score talked about prospects for the current Indians and then asked for questions. Two routine queries, and a hand goes up hesitantly: "Herb, what happened with McDougald?" Nineteen years later and they still ask. A pitcher with extraordinary skills loses them and people still wonder.

Six no-hitters and three perfect games in three years of high school ball, a total of eight hits allowed his entire junior year, brought scouts from 14 of the then-16 major league teams to his family's home. Ten offered bonuses up to $80,000 if he would sign with them; four said simply, "Tell us your best offer and we'll top it."

Herb and his mother had very little money but passed up the dollar hunt and chose a friend instead. Cy Slapnicka, the man who had signed Feller as a 17-year-old in Iowa, wintered in Score's hometown of Lake Worth, Florida. Told by a city cop one day about a freshman at Lake Worth High, Slapnicka went to watch—and kept his seat behind home plate for three seasons. Major league rules prevented him from talking contract until the youngster turned 19; but he could talk about other things, couldn't he? He could take Herb, his mother and two sisters out to dinner now and then. And, if the talk got around to baseball, he might mention a few of the nice things about the people he worked for. There's no law against that, is there?

So Slap and the family became genuinely great friends. And by the start of Herb's junior year, when the other scouts began to show in packs, it really was too late. (Even though Herb coincidentally had been dating the pretty daughter of one of them.) Slap offered $60,000. Herb took it, bought his mother a house and himself a record player.

Baseball was more than a game to Score, however talented he was; it was—well, it was communication. He was—still is—shy and modest. But intense, too, if that doesn't seem contradictory. "The reason I played so hard at baseball," he says, "was because that was the one thing *I could do*, the only thing that would lift me out of the crowd. We had no money. People knew my father drank a lot and someone would come by and say your father's down there somewhere drunk. My parents separated. We moved to Florida and sports was the only way I could 'say' something."

Some intangible within Score forced him to make his "statement" clear and sharp. "Players, great players, come to the majors all the time with extraordinary talent," says Rocky Colavito, Score's friend, teammate, and later, a coach, "but often they try to get by with just their God-given skills. I never saw any pitcher come up with the natural equipment Herb had, but that wasn't enough for him. He made perfect seem like second-rate. He had a burning desire to excel. In warm-ups he didn't jog, he ran. In playing catch along the sidelines, he didn't lob. He threw. Even after he won a game, he talked to me for hours about how *he* might have played better. He wouldn't accept an average performance."

No one could ever suggest that Score was not giving his best. In Indianapolis, manager Kerby Farrell walked out to the mound to remove Score after he had walked three successive batters. "Herb," he said, "you're not trying to relax." Score didn't hear the last two words and snapped, "Get away from me before I push your nose through your face." Score left the game and put the runway to the locker room into temporary eclipse by breaking every light bulb en route. Then he tore the locker room apart. Suddenly, Herb realized what he had done. From that point he kept his furies to himself. "If I don't pitch well, why should I take it out on other people?" he told me. "Why should people have to walk carefully around me?" No one, in the ballpark or at home, ever saw him angry again. When he was displeased with the way he pitched, he would wait until he got into his car after the game, roll up the windows and scream at the top of his voice.

In demand from his first year in Cleveland as a speaker at sports affairs, Score was politic and always said what the audience wanted to hear. But there was one exception. At a high school dinner, the baseball coach preceded Score and said that while the team had not done too well, "We all had fun." Score, always slow to criticize, had to disagree. "I don't understand how you could have fun while you were losing. I'll tell you honestly, it kills me."

Every batter was Herb's personal antagonist. "Every hit against me was a slap in my face," he says. "I hated that batter." Score can't remember those he got out, but he will give you---30 years later— clinical details of everyone who hit him going back to high school. He didn't walk too many in those days because high school kids scare. They see a wild fastballer, take three strikes and sit down, relieved they're still whole.

At that, perhaps they weren't too different from major leaguers. Frank Frisch, manager and second baseman of the Cardinals, watched a fast, wild Feller warm up before pitching against the Cards in an exhibition game in 1936. After one of Feller's errant pitches splintered a section of the backstop, Frisch called rookie Lynn King.

"Young man," he asked, "have you ever played second base?"

"No sir," King replied.

"Well, you're playing there today."

Feller struck out eight men in the first three innings of that game. One of them was shortstop Leo Durocher. Durocher looked at the first two strikes and, as legend has it, turned and walked away.

"Wait a minute," the umpire said. "You have another strike coming."

"Thanks," said Durocher. "I don't want it."

Score could have come directly to the Indians when he signed his contract in June 1952, but there were Wynn, Lemon and Garcia, each winning 20 games a year or more, and Feller, fading but good for 10 or 15 wins a season. Lopez wanted Score to pitch regularly and get over his wildness. In the closing months of the '52 season, Score went to Indianapolis, the Indians' top farm club, and walked 62 in 62 innings. He was demoted to Reading. There the next year, he walked 126 in 98 innings (and during warmup one day badly dented a new car waiting alongside the first baseline to be given away).

The Indians brought Score back to Indianapolis for spring training in 1954 and turned the matter over to Ted Wilks, the old Cardinal reliever who was then the Indianapolis pitching coach. Wilks' style was unusual. He swore a lot. From the dugout in full earshot of two city blocks: "Keep your damn head level. Watch the goddamn plate. Look where you're throwing if you want the ball to get there."

A pitcher's motion is a many-faceted and fragile thing. Every part of the motion—kick, step, release, follow-through—must be synchronized if the ball is to get where the pitcher wants it, to a piece of a strike zone 17 inches wide. Before Wilks, Herb just leaned back as far as he could behind a high leg kick to get as much "body" into each throw as possible. But the kick pulled his head back so he lost sight of catcher, plate and batter. His head bobbed as he came forward. After Score released the ball, his hard delivery carried him so far forward that his left elbow slammed into his right knee. In self-defense, he had long before strapped a rubber pad to his knee.

Wilks lowered Score's leg kick considerably. He taught Score to pivot, to get his power by swiveling his hips rather than by tilting backward as much as he had. And to keep his eyes on the target until he released the ball. The follow-through wasn't changed much, however; Score frequently finished a pitch with his back turned to the plate. Score often had been hit by batted balls he never saw.

Herb remained with Wilks in 1954 and pitched Indianapolis to a pennant. He reduced his walks to 140 in 252 innings, acceptable by any measurement, struck out 330, won 22 games and lost only 5. He was hit hard in only one game all season, a 6–5 loss to Louisville. His other four losses: 2–1 twice, 1–0, 4–3. He was elected Most Valuable Player in the league as well as Rookie of the Year. *The Sporting News*, the sports bible, chose him the number-one player in the minor leagues.

Herb was extremely popular, too. He became an instant kid brother to many athletes whose careers had ended and were hanging on perhaps for another year or two. During Herb's first visit to Indianapolis, a former major league pitcher named Johnny Hutchings was a coach. Herb, extremely thin, always had trouble with his uniforms, especially the pants.

Because of his fierce windup, his socks and the bottom of each pant leg would fall down continually. Herb would spend much of each ball game pulling up his trousers and socks. One afternoon, Hutchings called time out, picked up a roll of tape, and walked out to the mound. A huge man, weighing well over 300 pounds, Hutchings bent over laboriously, pulled up one of Herb's pant legs, then pulled up the sock, taped the sock to the pant leg just above the calf, adjusted the pant leg, did the same with the other leg, pulled the trouser leg and sock up, taped it, adjusted it. All in slow motion. When he finished, he stepped back a pace or two to survey his work, then walked up to Herb, took off Herb's cap and kissed him on the cheek. (When Hutchings died 10 years later, his will asked that Herb be a pallbearer.)

Gossip in spring training is almost as much a part of that annual ritual as baseball itself. Two hundred and seventy-two minor leaguers were in camps in 1955—Elston Howard, Most Valuable Player in the International League the year before, and Ken Boyer among them— trying to win a spot in the majors. But it seemed most of the sportswriters were looking at the quiet lefthander from Indianapolis who was not yet old enough to vote.

In the hierarchy of baseball players, the fastballer stands first— higher than the Ruths, Aarons and Gehrigs. Brains can create a crafty pitcher, even a junk ball hurler who wins by virtue of experience and guile and, maybe, an occasional spitter. But a fireballer is nature's gift. And baseball men stand in awe. Dazzy Vance, an excellent speedballer in his own right, was warming up one day near the end of his career to pitch an exhibition against Feller, just 17. A photographer came up to Vance and asked if he would mind posing with the young kid. "Ask him," said Vance, "if he would mind posing with me." Hierarchies within hierarchies. Herb Score fit. He, with the classic overhand fireball delivered almost javelin-like with the full stretch of his six-foot-two body.

A natural pitching motion or a batter's natural swing can exceed for pure beauty most things created by man. John McGraw ordered 16-year-old Mel Ott not to take any hitting advice even though Ott swung with his forward foot up in the air. Lopez told Score he'd fine him if he ever saw Herb comparing pitching styles with the other men on the team. When Herb experimented one day with a change-up ball, a new pitch, Lopez threatened to send him back to Indianapolis.

At the Indians' camp in Tucson that spring in 1955, Score pitched as if he feared he would be cut. His reputation as a perfectionist had preceded him. Coaches watched to see that he didn't drive himself too hard. Score admitted to one writer that he "didn't know how to throw easy. Every batter is tough for me. I even bear down on the pitcher."

Herb had one goal—formed back in Rosedale, N.Y. when he was in eighth grade—and he didn't want to lose it now. He didn't have to worry. Cleveland couldn't keep him in the minors any longer. The club had won 111 games and the pennant in 1954 with Wynn, Lemon and Garcia winning 55 games among them and Feller contributing 13. Could Score crack that starting rotation? He could and Lemon soon was moved to coin a couplet of sorts: "There's no big four any more/ Score's got to stay in the store."

The lefthander became the Indians' most effective pitcher that season. He struck out 245 batters in 227 innings—an average 9.70 for nine innings—breaking a 44-year-old record for rookies set by Grover Cleveland Alexander. No previous pitcher, not even Feller, had ever been able to strike out batters at that pace for a full season. Feller's best was 7.3, Walter Johnson's, 6.9. Score allowed only 2.85 earned runs per game, won 16 games and lost 10. Once again, he was voted Rookie of the Year. He pitched a one-hitter, a two-hitter, three three-hitters and struck out 16 batters in one game, only two less than the record of the time, 18, held by Feller. During one game in 1955, Detroit somehow successfully intercepted all of Herb's pitching signals, yet still lost, 3–1.

The following year was even better. Score won 20 and lost 9. He struck out 263—setting an unofficial freshman-sophomore record of 547—and brought his walks down to an average five per nine-inning game. He battled New York's Whitey Ford to the final days of the season for the earned-run title. Ford won with 2.47, .06 better than Score's. The Indian pitching staff slumped in 1956. Garcia was 11–12 and Feller was 0–4. "During the last half of the season," someone cracked, "Cleveland's big three were Score, Don Mossi and Ray Narleski." Mossi and Narleski were the Indians' relief pitchers. Even though the Indians lost the pennant to the Yankees by nine games, attention focused on Score during the last half of the season as he won 10 games and lost only one. Few pros had ever seen anyone who could pitch almost as hard and effectively at the end of a game as at the beginning.

Wilks, at Indianapolis, continued to monitor Score, in person when he could, other times on television. When the Indians came to Indianapolis for periodic exhibition games, Wilks would always meet Score at the airport, bellowing for all to hear, "You're not keeping your goddamn eyes on the batter."

At spring training in 1957, Mickey Mantle—who was to bat .365 that season—called Score the toughest pitcher he had ever hit against; the Boston Red Sox offered Cleveland $1 million cash for Score, the largest bid ever made for a ballplayer (the worth of the entire Cleveland franchise was estimated at $3 million); and *The Sporting News* asked, "Will Score become the greatest lefthander in the history of baseball?"

Four weeks later, Score's career effectively ended. It was his fourth start of the season, May 7, and he was in the first inning against the Yankees. He retired Hank Bauer and then came Gil McDougald, Yankee shortstop. With the count 2 and 2, McDougald had to swing at the fast ball belt high on the outside. He lined it back at the pitcher's mound. Score, as usual, had turned his eyes away in his follow-through. He looked up in time to see a flash of white before the ball hit him squarely in the right eye.

He crumbled, but never lost consciousness. He had remarkable presence of mind. He poked around in his mouth to see if he had swallowed his bridgework. Then he felt his ears to determine if he was bleeding from them. He knew he was bleeding badly; he could taste the blood in his mouth and from his nose. Colavito raced in from right field and then stood there, helpless. He finally put his glove under Score's head so Herb's face wouldn't have to be on the dirt.

The public address system announcer asked if there were any doctors in the stands; within minutes, six were at the pitcher's mound. Score was carried into the clubhouse and placed on the trainer's table. Pain, the real pain, hadn't started yet. By this time, the team's doctor, driving nearby, had heard of the accident on the radio and reached the ballpark. He got there in time to hear Herb crack, "Now I know how Fullmer felt last week." (Ray Robinson only days earlier had punched Gene Fullmer silly in a middleweight title bout.) At the end of the inning, Colavito raced to the clubhouse to find out how Score was doing and was greeted by mock anger: "What are you doing here? Get back to work." An ambulance brought Score to a hospital where an ophthalmologist was waiting.

Herb asked only one question, "Am I blind?" The physician, Dr. Charles I. Thomas, said, "I don't know. I can't tell the condition of your eye because it's swollen and hemorrhaging so badly." Drugs were administered to help stop the bleeding. Herb asked for a radio so he could listen to the rest of the game. (Cleveland won.)

Dr. Thomas made Herb lie still. He didn't want any pupil movement. He bandaged the left eye so Score wouldn't move that pupil which of course would cause the pupil in the right eye to move as well. Then the pain began, from the pressure in the right eye and from the fracture in his nose and a displaced right cheekbone.

Herb lay still for eight days. By then, the swelling around the eye had receded sufficiently so Dr. Thomas was able to have a clear field. The retina had been torn, but not completely. The physician hoped that surgery to repair the rip would not be necessary. Score would not be blind in that eye but might have a blind spot.

Three weeks later, he was discharged. His vision from the damaged eye was blurred for almost a year. No one knew if he would pitch again. Herb had been placed on large doses of cortisone and it took five months to wean him from that drug. He was finished with baseball for the balance of the season.

No one suggested to Score that he might not be able to come back from the injury, but there was concern. Herb had little depth perception; he couldn't tell if a ball thrown to him was three or 30 feet away. Exercises during the winter returned his depth perception to normal. Score asked Colavito to report early to spring training with him so he could pitch to Rocky with the usual waist-high batting-practice shield removed. Colavito was hesitant, but Herb, in his customary straight-out manner, said, "Rocky, I've got to know if I'm gun shy and now is as good a time as any." Colavito sprayed line drives and grounders throughout the infield and pitching area; Score didn't let up.

Herb lost his first game of the season but seemed to dispel all doubts in his second start, against the Chicago White Sox. He gave up two hits, struck out 14 and won, 3–0. "That convinced me," he said, "that I have everything I had before the accident."

He still hadn't regained his old pitching rhythm, but he wasn't worried. Spring that year was cold and rainy, not ideal conditions for a pitcher, especially one who had laid off for a year. Rain washed out what would have been Score's next two starts. Nine days later, he opened against the Senators on a damp, cold night. He was winning in the fourth inning when he attempted a curve and felt a strain in his forearm just below the elbow. In the seventh inning, a fast ball failed to reach the batter. Actually bounced in front of the plate. Incredulously, Herb tried again; same result. Now his arm began to hurt. He called manager Bobby Bragan to the mound and told him what happened. Score left the game. Next morning, his arm was swollen so badly he could hardly get it through the sleeve of his coat.

He was examined by the Washington team's physician who told him to rest the arm for a few days. Five days later, Herb tried to throw again. The pain was unbearable. Score consulted the Indians' doctor. He advised him not to pitch for 10 days. After 10 days, the arm continued to hurt, but Score thought he could work the pain out by throwing.

Finally, Herb went to Johns Hopkins, one of the outstanding hospitals in the country. There, he was told that he had torn a tendon back in April against Washington. Again, Herb was told to rest the arm, this time for 30 days. He obeyed, then began to throw again, in warmups, in batting practice, trying to get his arm back into condition. He threw hard a couple of times and felt no pain. Bragan asked him if he thought he could finish the last three innings of a game in Washington. Score got nine consecutive batters out, six by strike-outs. On the last pitch of the game, Score felt a sharp stabbing pain in his arm again, this time accompanied by a popping sound in his elbow.

Again the arm blew up. Score rested several weeks, then began to throw. He could still break off his curve as effectively as ever but his arm hurt every time he attempted a fast ball. Anxious about the amount of time he had missed, he began to press. He modified his throwing motion slightly to end the pain from the fast ball and told Bragan he was ready to go.

Several days later, he was called in from the bullpen in the fourth inning against the Yankees. (Ironically, the first batter was McDougald, the first time they had faced each other since the accident.) Herb had nothing on the ball except a curve and a slow change of pace—the same pitch Lopez had banned angrily two years earlier. Score struck out

McDougald and finished the game without giving up any runs. But he knew he couldn't throw well.

The agony lasted the remainder of that season—he finished with 2 wins and 3 losses. "I had spent practically two full seasons without pitching," Herb said. "All that time, I was developing bad habits. When I tried to work, I favored my elbow. If I threw low in a certain way, I wouldn't strain my arm, but I lost my fluid motion and my rhythm and I never recovered it." At midyear in 1959, Score had won nine games and lost four, mainly by careful use of his curve and the change-up. He no longer had the looseness he had before. He was throwing as hard, but the ball was nowhere near as fast as it had been.

Yet, 9–4 at the All-Star midyear break; he wasn't doing too badly. Joe Gordon, the new manager, suggested cutting down Herb's full motion drastically. Herb put unfamiliar stresses on his arm. He became a sore-arm pitcher. As his confidence began to ebb, so did his remaining effectiveness. He didn't win another game that season and lost seven more.

Gordon and general manager Frank Lane gave up on Score. Indian management would not let Herb be traded to anyone but Lopez, his first-year manager who was then handling the White Sox. Lopez had been watching his former pitcher closely and had seen what he believed were flashes of the 1955 Score. Shortly before the 1960 season began, Score, age 27, went to the Sox.

"Of course, there was an element of selfishness to it," Lopez says. "I hoped to profit by having Herb make good with the White Sox. But I also had another motive. In all my years in baseball, I never met a finer man. I felt I might be able to help him."

Lopez, some said, brought the guesswork of handling a pitcher to an art form. Perhaps it was his training as a catcher. He had the uncanny ability, for example, to pull a pitcher out of a game before maximum damage was done. He seemed to *know* before a pitcher stayed a bit too long, before a fast ball failed to jump, before a curve started to roll, even before a man's spirit failed. He never asked a pitcher. And for some reason understood by none, he was usually right.

But Lopez had no magic for Herb. The ordeal was not to end.

Score started 22 games that year, finished only five. In six of those early games, he made it past the fourth inning only once. He twice put 12 runners on base in less than four innings. "I was throwing the ball well and the pain was gone. But I just couldn't hit a groove, get the ball over. When I did get it over, there wasn't that much on it." There were brief moments, even games, when "all of a sudden, it looked like it was coming back. Then—nothing." He began "aiming" the ball, placing too much emphasis on his arm in an attempt to get the ball where it should go; in the process, whatever "stuff" he had on the ball would disappear.

The next season was worse; Herb started five games, finished one. About midseason, Score opened a night game in Baltimore, pitched to five batters and allowed four runs before Lopez sent in another pitcher.

Neither Lopez nor Score had an easy answer. And, of course, there was none. Herb felt well, the best in years, he told Chicago writers. Why was he pitching so "lousy," as he put it?

Lopez suggested Herb go down to San Diego, then a minor league team, for several weeks. There he could work regularly, pitch every four days in rotation, something not possible with Chicago. Herb, after talking it over with Nancy, a classmate from Lake Worth High whom he had married in 1957, agreed.

So Score went to San Diego. "In my own mind, I knew that I would never be what I once was," he said afterward. "But I was hoping that I could still pitch reasonably well, still win." His delivery became a parody of what it had been. He kept getting extreme periods of wildness, worse than when he had been a rookie. His arm would come to a kind of halt at the end of the windup and he seemed to be pushing the ball.

The old natural motion when he just reared back and threw now was replaced with constant planning. He explained it to writer Jack Olsen: "If I throw the ball and I haven't followed through or I land wrong, this would tell me that I'm not throwing right and I would say to myself, 'Let me pivot a little slower, let me bring my arm up higher,' and these are things you don't normally have to think about. You should get the sign from the catcher; then the only thing you should think about is I'm gonna throw this fast ball low and across the inside and concentrate only on that. But I would wind up and tell myself, 'Now make sure you pivot right, don't lean back too far, hold your head level,' and you can't do all that. And then I get behind a batter, maybe two balls and no strikes, and I begin to aim. I'd be better off if I just slung the ball and it wound up in the grandstand."

One holiday in San Diego, Score started the first game of a doubleheader against Seattle. He faced 11 batters in two innings, gave up two home runs, a double, two singles and walked three. He was brought in to relieve in the fourth inning of the second game. Seattle reached him for two singles, two doubles, two triples and six runs. In four innings, the pitcher who was to surpass Grove had given up 13 runs. In 133⅔ innings at San Diego, he walked 136, made 15 wild pitches, allowed 103 hits.

He went to the minors twice more after San Diego. In 1962 and again in 1963, he attempted a comeback with Indianapolis where he had started. He would not quit until he was sure he had given himself the time he needed. "I didn't want to think 15 years later that I could have pitched if I had tried a little longer. I went out and proved I couldn't pitch." *Then* it was time to stop.

"I'm grateful to have played in the major leagues and to have had some degree of success," he told reporters then. "I'm retiring sooner than I wanted to. That's nothing to be sad about."

As a measure of the respect men throughout baseball had for him, he was immediately asked to come back to Cleveland to broadcast its games. And that seemed fine to him. Because he loved baseball and now could stay with it.

Many skilled athletes have legends created about them: Williams, full of self-generated demons but, often, as gentle as a child; Cobb, noisy, hostile and cruel; Koufax, shy and private but extraordinarily principled. Score, too, created a legend quite apart from his ballplaying: a good man with the potential for athletic greatness who didn't complain when the vision died young. Lopez, his first—and last—major league manager may have said it best: "Herb, if my son was to be a baseball player, you're the one I'd want him to model himself after."

Courage is an ill-defined term. Certainly, it is not the exclusive property of athletes who come back from problems to their former renown. It belongs, too, to those like Score who labor with little success for six years in the hope they may find some part of their former brilliance. Score found none and who is to blame it on the eye injury or the torn tendon? Who even cares? He could have quit many times and none would have raised a voice against him. I know many athletes, in a variety of sports, who have quit for less—and demanded public sympathy as well.

What must it be like to realize that an eighth-grade dream—a reality well into manhood—is perishing? Within the context of sports, Herb's story is one of the saddest I know. Talent so great should wither gracefully so the rest of us can prepare for the end of something bestowed on few. One talks now to Herb and Nancy and expects to find—what? Disappointment—certainly. Bitterness—possibly. After all he was "sure" to make the Hall of Fame. He began pitching when salaries were just beginning to rival those of movie starlets. Not small losses. Yet he laughs when I suggest fate played a poor trick on him and turns the topic to something else.

Long after Herb went into decline, he was pitching the second game of a doubleheader against the Red Sox. It was late in the season, the temperature was about 94° and neither team was going anywhere in the pennant race. Score had absolutely nothing on the ball. Pitching just by instinct, he kept the Sox scoreless. His team managed a run to go ahead, 1–0, entering the ninth inning. Score got the first two batters out.

Ted Williams no longer played the second game of doubleheaders, but now he came in to pinch-hit. Score was perspiring, sick about the season he was having and struggling with every pitch. He got two strikes on Williams. Always an overhand pitcher, Score experimented with a side arm curve and, because of his fatigue or maybe his sweaty fingers slipped, the ball took a couple of unexpected dips. Williams stared at it—the pitch was a long time getting to the plate—and he finally swung as if he had an axe in his hand, almost straight down, and he missed.

Score didn't know it, but that was the last shut-out he would pitch in the majors. His arm was dead and hurting and he knew it was a matter of time before he would have to stop playing. But on that hot Sunday in Boston with absolutely nothing at stake he had to win.

Pete Reiser, the old Dodger outfielder, would understand that. Reiser crashed into so many outfield walls trying to catch long drives that he shortened his career considerably. One July afternoon in 1942, Brooklyn was leading the league by 13½ games and the Cardinals were in town. It was the second game of a doubleheader, there was no score and it was in extra innings. Enos Slaughter belted a ball deep to centerfield. Racing for it, Reiser thought, "If I don't get it, it's a triple and there could go the game."

He slammed into the wall at full speed, dropped the ball and knocked himself out. In the hospital, he learned he had a fractured skull, "Was I being foolhardy in going after that ball the way I did?" Reiser asked years later. "After all, we had a 13½ game lead.... You can slow up in those circumstances, can't you? No, you can't. You slow up a half step and it's the beginning of your last ball game. You can't turn it on and off any time you want to. Not if you take pride in yourself."

On the morning that Herb's and Nancy's second child was delivered—with Down's syndrome—Herb had been scheduled to speak before a father and son Communion breakfast at their church. He didn't want to go, but Nancy insisted. Those who were there said Herb spoke without notes, without mentioning what had happened that morning—no one there knew until later. He spoke longer than he usually did. Quietly, he spoke of family, of love, of doing one's best at whatever one does and of accepting what life offers without complaint. He could have been thinking of the daughter who the next day would be christened Susan Jane; he could also have been thinking of an arm that mysteriously died. Those who were there said no talk of Herb's ever moved them more.

END

Rocky Bleier

If you believe in numbers, he should have been a lawyer, maybe an insurance salesman. Because the figures were terrible.

It was January 7, 1968, and teams of the National Football League were choosing the college players they wanted to hire. Rocky Bleier was not at the head of anyone's list. As a matter of fact, he wasn't even on most lists.

With thousands of athletes pouring out of colleges each year, the pros need some orderly way to rate and eventually pick those few, of the thousands, they would like to add to their rosters.

Long before selection time, teams give players points for their weaknesses, their deficiencies. For example, if John Fiercelooking of the University of Wherever can't catch a ball, that's a problem—and he gets a bundle of points. And, months later, when draft time arrives and a team wants to know how it rated John, it asks its computer and out pops a figure. Fiercelooking's football days are over.

The *worst* rating possible is 2.5. Above 1.8, the player "is not capable of playing pro ball." Bleier was judged from 2.2 to 2.4. Wait. It gets worse. One Bleier observer noted: "… can't win in the NFL with this kid." Another: "I don't think this boy can make a pro club."

But Rocky had some "intangibles" where the Pittsburgh Steelers were concerned. Things they couldn't put into the machine. For example, one coach said "heart." Tell that to a computer programmer. So when the Steelers, a club that had won four of 14 games in 1967, got down to the bottom of its computer, that coach raised his voice a little and asked something like, "How do you measure heart?" and Bleier got picked. He was number 417 of 441 men finally selected by the NFL.

The Steelers picked 18 players that year. Bleier, number 18, is the only one still in pro ball.

The army drafted Rocky before his rookie year with Pittsburgh ended and sent him to Vietnam. Nine months later, he was returned: his right foot was a half shoe-size smaller than his left; the bottom of that foot had been ripped open by shrapnel along the instep from heel to ball, across the big toe and the second toe; the second toe was splintered. Dozens of pieces of shrapnel had pierced his right leg from his foot to his thigh.

Bleier, a disarmingly honest man, is equally candid with God. As he lay behind clumps of bushes in South Vietnam, wounded, weapon gone, close enough to the enemy to hear them, well aware their machine gun could cut through the growth and kill him, wondering if his small, cut-off group would be overrun, he prayed: "Dear Lord, get me out of here if you can. I'm not going to bullshit you. I'd like to say that if you get me out of here alive and okay, I'll dedicate my life to you and become a priest. I can't do that because I know that's not what I'll do. I don't want to promise anything now and then change my mind later when things are going good. I don't want to come to you with a tight-situation prayer if I can't be honest. What I will do is this. I'll give you my life ... to do with whatever you will.... I'm not going to complain if things go wrong. If things go good, I'll share my success with everybody around me. Whatever you want to do, wherever you want to direct me, that's fine. This is the best I can do."

A grenade had exploded at Bleier's feet. A steel plate built into army combat boots was the only reason he still had a right foot. Muscle and flesh also had been ripped from his left thigh by small-arms fire.

What are you going to do when you get back to civilian life, Rock?

"I'm a football player, aren't I?"

Well, maybe not. Maybe not when the army lists you officially as 40 per cent disabled. And the disability affects as important a part of you as the sole of a foot. A running back has to start, and push off from, a three-point stance—crouched and leaning on one hand and the toes and balls of both feet. Pushing off is a fundamental move for a runner. It allows him to start quickly and change direction sharply.

Calcium deposits that form around broken bones and scar tissue had, in effect, "frozen" the first two toes and adjacent ligament and muscle areas of Bleier's right foot. The toes would not bend, forward or backward. In addition, muscles on the ball of the right foot had begun to atrophy.

The injuries to the right foot would be Bleier's major obstacle. The other wounds would heal even though infection had invaded as high as his calf. An operation by army surgeons attempted to cut out the scar tissue and bone spurs in the hope it—and later physical therapy—would allow Bleier to regain the flexibility and strength he once had there. The operation was only partially successful. Therapy did little, even electrical stimulation therapy in which a technician shocked the bottom of Bleier's right foot trying to induce movement in his toes was unsuccessful.

Play again?

An army physician in a Tokyo hospital was the first in line: "Rocky, it's impossible." His old coach at Notre Dame, Ara Parseghian, was next although Ara couldn't bring himself to tell Rocky directly: "He's had half his foot shot away. You need your hip, knee and ankle in perfect shape just to walk. Even with a little blister, you can't run. Here he's had all the ligaments, tendons and muscles damaged. I just hope he'll be able to walk normally."

When the wounds healed, Bleier began to work out by himself. He was on light duty at Fort Riley, Kansas. His injuries looked mended, he thought. So they must *be* mended. He thought he would just jog a couple of miles the first day. An easy, slow start.

At about a half mile, he collapsed, "... crying in deep, convulsive sobs as I gasped for air. My mind was racing in disbelief. After all those years as an athlete—my body skilled, strong, responsive—I was now a physical disaster, My foot hurt, my heart was pounding, I couldn't breathe and I lay there, with training camp three months away. Will I ever play football again?"

Bleier *couldn't* run. He couldn't walk. He couldn't put his foot down in any position without extreme pain. He was limping badly. He felt what seemed to be a sharp stone in his right shoe, but he couldn't find it.

Bleier devised an inner-sole device that made it possible to run on that right foot without agony and put himself on a murderous schedule: up at 5:30 A.M. to run outdoors near his off-base apartment, report to his duty assignment at 7:00, lift weights at the post gym from 6:00 to 8:00 P.M., drive back to his apartment, run sprints on the lawn for an hour, shower and go to bed. For five days a week, for three months, that was Bleier's life. He didn't miss an exquisite moment of it.

Bleier ran frequently against roommate Steve Eller, who outweighed

Rocky by some 70 pounds. Rocky couldn't beat a man who was not an athlete and who was far from a perfect physical specimen.

"When I did beat the SOB," Rocky told me much later, "it would be by perhaps a step in the 40-yard-dash. And Eller would stick the knife in: 'You're a football player? If I were in shape, I'd beat the ass off you.' He was right. The refrain reverberated within my skull: 'You're an athlete? You're an athlete?' The only way I could 'answer' was to run more."

As Bleier's foot began to hurt less, he and Eller ran up and down the steps at Kansas State University's football stadium, one of the most torturous stunts ever devised for man. Bleier reached the point where he could run up and down, bottom to top, full-out, five consecutive times with 10-pound weights tied to each ankle.

Discharged in July 1970, Bleier moved in with former Notre Dame teammate Terry Hanratty and Terry's wife Rosemary in Pittsburgh. The first NFL player strike was on and Bleier stayed out of preseason training camp with the other Steeler veterans. Hanratty took one look at Bleier and began to worry. ("You're really limping, Rock." "What the hell's the matter with you? I'm not limping.") Hanratty became concerned.

"Rock," he said, "you know the team's a lot different now than it was in '68." (A new coach, Chuck Noll, had been hired in 1969. He was to sweep through the Steeler team that greeted him. Only five were left by Super Bowl time, 1974.)

"Yeah."

Bleier had talked at Notre Dame of becoming a lawyer and Hanratty reminded him. "You've been thinking of law. Take the entrance exams this fall. Maybe you should quit. You sure as hell don't need this."

Rocky didn't get angry. Hanratty was a very close friend. "I'd like to give it a shot, Terry, and see what happens."

Bleier asked the team veterans at a meeting in early August if he could report to training camp because of his special reconditioning needs and the players agreed. Rocky had only one goal for the '70 season: rejoin the club. He didn't care how he rejoined the team; a spot on the taxi squad would do (with the players under contract who practice with the team but aren't included on the official roster and can't play in league games). He didn't care if he played. He didn't want to be "out of sight, out of mind" for two seasons.

Nine running backs were in camp, including Bleier. They were competing for five spots. Dick Hoak and Earl Gros were the only backs remaining from 1968, Rocky's rookie year. Two had joined as rookies in 1969: Warren Bankston of Tulane and Don McCall of Southern California. Two came on trades during the '69–'70 off-season: Frenchy Fuqua from the Giants and Preston Pearson from the Colts.

Training camp is a brutal time, physically and emotionally. Past records mean nothing. The best players make the ball club. It's not a personality contest. It's a vicious battle for a job and even a wounded Vietnam veteran can expect no special consideration.

Bleier's foot was hurting and he was limping steadily. (He thought he was not and could not be persuaded until much later that, in fact, he had limped badly with every step, walking or running, during all of training camp.) He had gotten his weight up from 160 to where it had been, 200, but his speed—rather, lack of it—shook him during the first 40-yard sprints. His best as a rookie in uniform was perhaps 4.8 seconds. His untimed victories in Kansas over Eller had given him false confidence; for he was now, in camp, running close to 6 seconds, out of the question for a pro at *any* spot, even the biggest lineman.

He was running flatfooted, using the outside edge of his right shoe. (He still runs that way today.) He couldn't get up on his toes. The equipment man did what he could. He put a bar under Rocky's right shoe, hoping he could push off that way when starting, rather than use his toes. He removed a cleat from under the big toe on the right foot, hoping to relieve painful pressure on the toe. Nothing worked. Bleier wrapped his right foot in extra tape and socks, especially during exhausting two-a-day practices that drain even the best conditioned players.

Bleier had convinced himself that he was improving, was getting faster, growing stronger, becoming more impressive. All not true. He became the cause of heated debates. Art Rooney, Jr., a vice-president, told his brother Dan, Steeler's president: "The kid's going to get hurt. A back can't be *taking* all the blows. He's got to be *giving* them. Rocky can't protect himself. One of these afternoons when he's really tired, he's going to get killed."

Dr. John Best, the Steelers' orthopedic surgeon, agreed: "He can't go, Danny. He just can't go." From the equipment man: "I can't stand by and watch him go through any more." From the trainer: "Rocky won't quit on his own. It's not human ... to let him endure any more pain."

Backfield coach Max Coley spoke privately to Bleier. "Football's just not that important, Rock. It's only a small part of your life. It's not worth it if you're going to be permanently damaged."

Bleier played little during the preseason exhibition games. A week before the season was to start, it was time for the final cut. (NFL teams then could carry 47 players. Hopefuls were eliminated during the preseason training.) Noll sent for Bleier.

Noll's an unemotional pragmatist. The message was blunt. "Rock, we put you on final waivers. We think you'll pass through" (i.e., not be selected by another club). Final waivers offers a player to any club for $100 before his team releases him outright. Clearly, no team would want Bleier if the Steelers didn't. "Get yourself into shape. Then you can come back next year."

Rocky's goal—stay with the club *somehow*—was dying.

Bleier is neither unemotional nor, at that moment, was he outstandingly pragmatic. He argued. "Coach, can't I be sent to the taxi squad or something? I feel good. I can help. I don't want to lose the whole season." Bleier tried for another moment, then turned to leave. What can you say after you've been fired?

"As I began to walk out," Rocky said, "Chuck showed a crack in his impenetrable exterior for the first and only time in my experience. His voice softened a tone and he said, 'If you want, you can practice with us today.'"

Everyone on the team knew Bleier had been cut, yet—a workout was waiting. Rocky Bleier doesn't miss workouts. Even when they're for nothing. He suited up and worked out. Then he left. He was the final man of 25 cut.

Driving home, Bleier was alternately storming and crying. "For the first time since fifth grade, I wasn't a football player any more."

Then a rare force entered Bleier's life. It was a 69-year-old man who had owned a football team for 39 years and never saw it win even a division title. No pro football owner has yet been suggested for sainthood, but Arthur Rooney, Sr., someday will sit at the right hand of St. Peter, cigars and all.

Bleier received a phone call the morning after he had been cut. Dan Rooney would like to see him. Dan hadn't read the waiver list until late the previous evening. He told his father. His father wondered if another operation on his right foot would help Rocky. Dan, in fact, had suggested that to Bleier at the very start of training camp, but eager to get with the team, Bleier had declined. Dan then asked Noll if he would mind if Bleier were put on the injured reserve list. He couldn't play but he would be with the team unofficially and not take up one of the playing spots. Noll agreed.

When Bleier got to Dan's office, Dan told him of the proposed operation and suggested that Rocky could rejoin the team later in the season after recuperating. Bleier *would* remain a Steeler for the 1970 season.

Surgery was the following day. Dr. Best found and removed a small piece of shrapnel that had worked its way to the surface just below Rocky's fourth toe. That was the "sharp stone" he had been feeling. While Bleier was under anesthesia, Dr. Best with his hands simply ripped scar tissue apart in and around the other toes, freeing them and the ligaments and muscles in the area. Exercise would keep scar tissue from re-forming. For the first time since the grenade exploded, Bleier now had reasonable movement in his right toes.

An anticipated four-week recuperation took eight weeks but only three in bed. Mr. Rooney, Sr., told Art, Jr., to give Bleier some scouting assignments and said, "He might like it. If his foot doesn't get better, let's see if we can find a place for him." An employer owes a returning veteran 30 days work. No more. Bleier had been wounded in the army and his medical problems were the army's responsibility. Mr. Rooney, Sr., paid for the operation and gave Rocky a 25 per cent raise over his rookie salary.

Between infrequent scouting jobs, Bleier began working out on his own. By the eighth week, he was in uniform again, practicing with the team and attending meetings. By the final game of the season, two backs had been hurt and Noll reactivated Rocky so he could get into uniform and sit with the club on the field. Pittsburgh ended the season with five wins and nine losses.

Bleier took an apartment near Chicago, a job selling insurance, and a pledge he would be better when the 1971 season began. Again up at 6:00 to run slush-filled streets; sell insurance from 8:00 until 1:00; weights until 6:00; sell insurance until 9:00; sprints for an hour and bed. Bleier was alone in a new area and his only company was a recurring inner voice: *"Bleier driving over for the touchdown."* Fragile motivation for 6:00 A.M. on a winter's day in Chicago when no one is looking.

His insurance business suffered as Bleier agonized over his right foot and wondered if he could survive a second training camp when he was still far from ideal condition. He called the Steelers to ask if he could report early—with the rookies. He joked about his insurance work. Chuck Noll responded quietly: "Rock, if you've got something good going in Chicago, maybe it would be best if you didn't try to come back."

Bleier pushed away that kindness—and it was that—and received permission to report early. He continued to work out. And then, a week before he was to report, he pulled a hamstring muscle in his left leg just where bullets had cut out a piece of it.

He arrived at camp and, first day, ripped the injured hamstring. Out of action for three weeks. He would miss the most vital part of training camp for the marginal athlete trying to win a team spot—the two-a-day practices. Dr. Best had a talk with Bleier.

"What do you do in the offseason, Rock?"

"I sell insurance."

"Do you like it?"

"Yeah."

"You know, you were wounded in that left thigh. You lost a chunk of your leg. You're always going to have trouble with your hamstrings. I'm going to have to tell Dan and Chuck this. Think about insurance, will you." That last wasn't a question, not the way Dr. Best said it.

Several days later, Noll asked Bleier. "How's it feeling?"

"I don't know," Bleier said. "I think I need a little more time."

"I'm afraid we don't have much time. We have to start making some decisions about people."

Bleier didn't respond.

"Look, Rock, why don't you follow up on your insurance business? I think you should retire."

The team flew to Green Bay for an exhibition game. Bleier drove to his hometown, Appleton, Wisconsin, after the game, talked with his family and visited his old friend and high school counselor, Father Al Lison.

Bleier put out what he believed were his three options: (1) wait for the hamstring to heal completely; by that time, it might be too late in training camp to make the team; (2) continue to practice and pray it wouldn't pull again; and, (3) quit.

"Only one makes sense to me now, Al," he said. "Strap up the leg and go back to practice on Monday. If I pull it again, I pull it and I'm done. If I don't pull it, maybe I've got a chance."

Bleier returned to camp, wrapped the leg, and worked. The final cuts were coming. Five running backs were question marks. One would stay. One more might make the taxi squad. Three would go. His chances were slim.

The team played an exhibition against Cincinnati. One back was cut. An exhibition against Minnesota. Another running back was cut. Bleier was the only back who had not yet played. Then the Jets—and Bleier saw his first action of any kind since his rookie year with the Steelers. He went in halfway through the last quarter. He hurtled through a hole for four yards, scrambled through another for 16, caught a pass for six. A third running back was cut. Of the questionables, Bleier and another man were left.

Rocky then played briefly against the Giants and did little. The following Wednesday was final-cut day. En route home from New York, Bleier began to feel ill. By Pittsburgh, he was sick enough to go directly to a doctor. Acute tonsillitis.

Wednesday morning, Noll called Bleier in. "Rock, we put you on waivers. We think you'll pass through again. Once we see how your throat is, in a game or two, we'll reactivate you."

Bleier was quick-witted enough to say thank you and left. But he wondered. After trying to persuade him weeks earlier to retire, Noll had kept him. Why? Bleier now knew he had not yet shown Noll—anyone—evidence that he was a player to be kept on a club clearly building for a long-time stay at the top. He was upset by whispers that he was not released because he was Irish and from Notre Dame and a medal winner (Bronze Star and Purple Heart).

Limping with the still unhealed hamstring, Bleier heard the whispers and the outright talk and they hurt. He didn't want favors. The standout athlete in elementary school, an 11-letter winner in high school, the *captain* of Notre Dame's football team shouldn't need gifts. Yet he was still somewhat of a caricature of an athlete. Why *did* Noll keep him? "I was something less than a football player. Looking at the situation honestly, what club would have kept me once they saw I was of no immediate use?"

He later learned that backfield coach Max Coley, who the year before had suggested he quit, wanted Bleier. In a coaches' meeting before the '71 season opener against Chicago, Coley said, "Rocky's the only guy I have who will stick his nose in there and block Dick Butkus." When Bleier heard that, he said, "Sure I would have. Hell, that was *all* I could do."

Bleier played that year, eight games, in spite of pulling the injured hamstring again. All on special teams, termed suicide squads (selected athletes who form units solely for such situations as kickoffs, kickoff returns, field goal and extra point tries, punts and punt returns; their number and character vary from team to team). He still was not a player of pro caliber. He was still outside in a way, looking in. When you're hurt, when you're not contributing, even if it's only for a game or two, suddenly you're an outsider. These could be athletes you had played with for years, but you're not one of them. It's unspoken. But it's real. And it rubs a raw nerve. That's how Bleier felt during much of that on-again, off-again 1971 season.

But goal number two was accomplished. Bleier now was *on* the team. And that helped. The Steelers finished 6–8.

Back to suburban Chicago, insurance and reconditioning. He had to prove he was a hard-nosed pro who needed no considerations from anyone. The emphasis was on strengthening his right foot. He ignored the ever-present pain in the foot and started racing full-steam up and down the steps of his apartment building. He started with three floors up and down three times without stopping, then four up and down four times, then five, six, seven, eight. Eight floors, full-out, eight times up and down without stopping to die.

He did the stairs routine daily. He returned to his omnipresent weights. He added a half-hour to his schedule of the previous offseason. He got up at 5:30 instead of 6:00, squeezed in an afternoon workout as well. So he was now exercising three times a day—six days a week—instead of two. He also ran five 350-yard races daily in less than 60 seconds each and finished each day with sprints. He *had* to move faster, bad foot or not.

He went home for Christmas and discovered his 51-year-old father standing on his head. Bleier's father had taken up yoga and he was far more flexible than his son. Bleier couldn't touch his head to the floor while sitting on the floor; his father could. Rocky was still learning from his father. He bought a beginning yoga book. Perhaps the weight lifting had tightened his muscles, particularly in his legs. Would flexibility exercises added to the ever-present weight lifting and the running help?

He found out first day back at 1972 training camp. Everyone was being timed at 40-yard dashes. Three watches clicked and off went Bleier. He trotted back to find three coaches shaking their watches next to their ears, listening for broken parts. Bleier had been timed *faster* than his rookie year. One watch had 4.55. The slowest had 4.65—two-tenths of a second faster than he was before he was wounded. (This just shouldn't happen. Gil Brandt, the Dallas Cowboys' director of personnel, put it well. "No one ever gets faster in pro football," he once said. "You pick up a back who runs a 4.8 and maybe in a few years he'll be 4.9 and a few years later he'll be 5.0 and too slow to play.")

Why was Rocky faster? The foot still hurt.

Three years of work were beginning to pay off for the tough kid who wasn't supposed to be able to play pro ball when he was whole, was told to quit when he was wounded, and wasn't smart enough to listen to anyone. Three years of building strength into his legs and body, the extensive winter, spring and early summer of flexibility exercises—courtesy of Mr. Bleier, Sr.—and another intangible: he *wanted* to be faster.

"No question that by the offseason between '71 and '72 I was overcompensating," Bleier said. "I was studying sprinters' form to see how they ran, their arms, their legs, position of their feet. My own workouts almost daily pushed me beyond what I had thought my limits to be. I probably could have done half of what I did and improved my speed by 1972, but I didn't know that."

Goal number three was to play in '72. To show everyone he was there on his own merit. He did play—every game. By the time the year ended, with the Steelers 11–3 and a division winner for the first time in their history, Bleier was established—but only on special teams.

The fact that Bleier played every game didn't satisfy him. Bleier wanted to be a starter. He had carried the ball once during the season.

In the next offseason, in what had come to be Bleier's trials by self-imposed ordeals, he decided to build up his strength and bulk. Back to six days a week. Running and weight lifting continued. He began talking with professional body builders and picking their brains. He used the help also of two coaches Pittsburgh had just hired: Lou Riecke, a strength coach, and Paul Uram, a flexibility coach.

During the '72 season, following his yoga workouts, Rocky went through his first football season without injury. With Uram, the team's number of muscle pulls and serious leg injuries was cut by more than half. Bleier visited a physiologist and learned ways to better develop the leg muscles a cutting, dodging, accelerating running back needs most. Bleier's weight rose to 225, then slimmed to 216 rock-solid pounds when training camp for 1973 began.

This was the year, Bleier had told himself, in which he would "make" the team on his terms, as a running back.

His condition was superb. The team equipment manager changed his shoulder pads; Bleier was two sizes larger than as a rookie. Only two men on the team—both offensive line-men—were stronger than

Bleier. Only two were faster: wide receiver Frank Lewis and running back Steve Davis.

During the exhibition games, Rocky now was running. He led all the backs in average yards-per-carry when the season began. But during the final exhibition game, he hurt his knee. By the time his knee mended, Franco Harris, Pittsburgh's number-one runner who also had been hurt, was back. Bleier returned to special teams.

He played on all six teams—kickoff and punt coverage, kickoff and punt return, field goal, and extra-point kicking. He was gaining fame as special-teams player. He was usually the first Steeler downfield and—blocking or tackling—used his body in more ways than nature intended. Television directors turned isolated cameras on him: Look what Bleier did now, folks.

But he remained the fifth and last running back in Noll's mind. Near the end of the year, Noll wanted better blocking on third downs and short yardage, on third and scoring position. He asked Dick Hoak, who had returned to the Steelers as backfield coach, who his best blocker was. Bleier, said Hoak, also mentioning—apparently unheard—that Bleier runs with the ball, too.

So Bleier went in perhaps six to eight times a game, usually to block, sometimes to carry, and was uncomfortable. "Not only are you coming in cold; you haven't been in long enough to know what the other team is doing; you put your reputation on the line during just a fraction of a game. Specialty teams are different; that's sort of a game within a game and it has its own 'rules.'" The Noll experiment soon ended.

The Steelers, picked by some as the dark horse favorite of the year, finished with 10–4 and a spot in the playoffs. Oakland eliminated them in the first game.

The following season, 1974, the year Pittsburgh was to win in the Super Bowl, began with Bleier beginning to think of himself as a journeyman ballplayer, one whom Noll considered only in terms of special teams.

The Players Association started the 1974 training camp by calling a strike. The Steelers' team representative had resigned. Preston Pearson succeeded and asked Bleier to help. He agreed. It didn't help his image.

"After what the Rooneys did for him, how could he turn on them?" Even Rocky's mother had a few tart words.

Art Rooney, Sr., heard the criticism and called Bleier: "Rock, I heard someone question your allegiance to the Rooneys. He said you owed us more loyalty than you're showing during this strike because we supposedly 'carried' you after your Vietnam experience. I just want to tell you that's not true. You've been an asset to us, both on and off the field. We don't want you to think you owe us anything. If you feel what you're doing is right, that's fine with me."

Bleier began to be assailed by doubts. It was, of course, possible that he was wrong and everyone else right. Should he quit? Should he keep to his torturous workouts? Were they going to get him somewhere? Bleier realized that at 28 he was getting old as far as special teams are concerned. He could easily be replaced by a rookie. And, because he now had five years in for a league pension, the club could consider him expendable.

During the exhibition period, Bleier was reduced to two specialty teams: kickoff and kick return. He logged minimal time as a running back. Franco Harris and Steve Davis started all the exhibition games.

The same pair started the season as running backs. Pittsburgh defeated Baltimore and tied with Denver. Harris hurt his leg. Frenchy Fuqua took over. The Steelers lost to Oakland.

A new running-back unit was formed in the last five minutes of the first half against Houston the next week. The Steeler offense was sputtering. Noll sent Bleier and Pearson in. The Steelers moved 39 yards and scored a field goal.

Bleier and Pearson started the second half. Bleier's blocking was superb. He gained 37 yards. Pearson ran for 117. Pittsburgh won, 13–7.

Kansas City was next; Noll stayed with his new running combination. It was Bleier's first start in the NFL. Pittsburgh won again, 34–24. Bleier scored his first touchdown. He gained 45 yards running and 45 more on pass receptions. He was the Steeler's high man in total offense.

Pearson and Bleier started against Cleveland the following week. The Steelers won their third consecutive game.

Now Harris was ready to play again. Bleier had been playing Franco's position, fullback. Noll moved Rocky to halfback in spite of the fact that he had not run a play from halfback all season. Bleier would start with Harris against Atlanta.

That game proved to be the pivotal one of the season for the Steelers and for Bleier. The offense—including a line that had been changing from week to week as the coaching staff sought the best combination—finally jelled. Harris and Bleier both set career highs rushing, Franco, 141 yards, and Rocky, 78. (To put that 78-yard total in perspective, Bleier had gained only 70 yards total, including his 1968 rookie year, until that game.) Bleier scored one of Pittsburgh's three touchdowns.

His blocking was deadly efficient. It was to be instrumental in helping Harris gain 881 yards running in the last nine regular season games and 512 yards and six touchdowns in the playoffs.

Many things went into Bleier's blocking success: his strength, courtesy of all those offseasons spent lifting weights; his leverage because he was smaller than most everyone on the field; and his desire, articulated at Notre Dame by assistant coach Tom Pagna: "Blocking is just a lot of wanting to." Noll began to call Bleier his "third guard."

Franco and Rocky started again the following week and the Steelers shut out Philadelphia. Against Cincinnati, Rocky pulled the Achilles tendon in his left foot. The Steelers lost. Bleier sat out much of the next two games. Pittsburgh defeated Cleveland again, then New Orleans. Bleier thought he was back on the bench to stay. Houston followed and the offense fell apart. Bleier went back in. Pittsburgh lost, 13–10, the last game it was to lose in 1974. Bleier stayed in the lineup as Pittsburgh defeated New England and Cincinnati.

Against Buffalo in the first playoff game, he gained 99 yards running and receiving as the Steelers won, 32–14. A 27-yard touchdown pass, Bradshaw to Bleier, put Pittsburgh in front to stay in the second quarter, 10–7. Oakland was next and lost to the Steelers, 24–13. Harris ran for 111 yards and Bleier gained only 13 less rushing and 25 on passes. (As late in the season as that game, football writers noted "surprise" at Bleier's play.) The game's turning point came early in the fourth quarter when Pittsburgh drove 61 yards in nine plays to tie the score. All but one of those plays were on the ground by Harris and Bleier. Bleier's 23-yard run was the longest in that series.

The 1975, 1976, 1979 a nd 1980 Super Bowls were anticlimactic for Bleier. His running and blocking were parts of a superb machine. Of the starting Pittsburgh team in all four Super Bowls, no one had been rated as poorly as Bleier. His fellow backs, for example, Terry Bradshaw and Franco Harris, were 0.9 and 1.0, respectively.

Monuments. The world is filled with things built to honor this event or that person. Someone might make a case for "monuments" within people. Bleier is a monument of the kind of God-given intensity some fools call stupidity. Out of the debris that was Bleier in 1970 emerged a running back on a four-time world championship football team. And no one except Bleier anticipated that. Who said God doesn't talk to Notre Dame men?

END